Dedications

To Alex and Alaya, someday you'll read this diary, and I hope you realize that this was your home before you ever walked through the door. God brought you here and we are thankful every single day for that fact. No matter what life brings to us, Mom, Sissy and I all love you, "SOOOO much!!"

Tori, I want you to remember this journey and how wonderfully supportive you were in the process. You really are an incredible person and the best big sister anyone could ask for.

To all of our friends and family that walked the path beside us, we thank you. Your love and support then and now, is amazing. We are honored to have you in our lives, and our kids are blessed to share in your love.

Finally to Holly, thank you for the idea of a blog, the nudge to keep it evolving, your honest feedback, and the editing support. Without you, this book would have never happened.

Our kids are blessed to have all of this love and support, as are we.

We love you all!

To the reader:

When we first toyed with the decision of adopting through foster care, I could not find any real candid explanation of what to expect. This book started as an open letter to our friends and family and has grown into so much more. Like this story we have grown into a strong loving family that is smart enough to count our blessings.

As a trans-racial family, we are dealing with anything that pops up, and teaching each other along the way. Together there is nothing we cannot do. If you would like to continue following our adventure check out our blog at http://thankyoufostercare.blogspot.com/

There are so many children in need of a loving and supportive family. If you are considering foster care and/or adoption, I hope you find this informative and helpful.

Thank you,
Tom

1. Our back story... March 24, 2009

Sonya and I are blessed to have a beautiful nine-year-old daughter, Tori. We have been married for ten years now and live in the house of our dreams. Life is good....

The back story

Sonya re-entered my life when I was dealing with my new knee injury and on worker's comp. At the time I lived with my friend Tim and his soon-to-be bride, Erika. I had retreated into that house and shut out many of the people in my life. While hanging out with "the boys," I invited my friend Jen over. She brought Sonya with her. Sonya and I had met each other before, but we had not really talked outside of casual discussion in a group setting. To say that we hit it off is a huge understatement. We spent that day and many after just talking and laughing. During our famous discussions that would last for hours, we discussed our dreams and plans. We both wanted to have a child and then adopt a second. Two months later, I asked her parents if I could have her hand, they gave me the whole darn package. :)

Well, a year later we were married and living in our first house when the great news came that we were going to have a baby. I spent the next nine months asking a million questions (the OB/GYN offered to drop his normal rate and charge me by the question) of everyone. After many false alarms, the time finally came. I rushed Sonya to the hospital, and several hours later our loved ones were holding the most beautiful baby I had ever seen. I cried for three days and still have no idea why. I think I had something in my eye.

Our life changed in the small delivery room. Gone were the weekends at the bar, or nights out at the movies. We replaced all of that with a rediscovery of the world through the eyes of our new little girl, which felt way cool. Everything that 'stopped' for us was replaced with ten new, even better things. Sonya laughed at me when I slept in the floor of Tori's room when she had her first cold; yet Sonya checked on us ten times that night.

During the course of the next nine years, our life has just kept getting better. I found a great career (that I still enjoy today). Through Tori we have re-learned how to walk, talk, and have our first real day at school, all while learning to see the best in everything again.

We decided we wanted another child. While researching adoption we became very concerned (mainly about the cost and timing), so we decided we would try for another one. We pulled the goalie. Soon after, we had another positive test! Yahoo!!!!

Then a month later, on the day of the first doctor's appointment, we suffered a miscarriage. Just after we announced the happy pregnancy news to everyone, we had to share this awful miscarriage news. We were crushed. If not for our two-year-old angel Tori, who knows what could have happened. We worked through the sadness and decided to keep trying. Months went by with no success, but our approach of "it will happen if it is meant to" allowed us to enjoy every day.

Fast forward: Last summer we decided to buy our new house, so we packed up and moved to the country. Tori, armed with her new room and the ability to talk to our neighbor's horses, has changed yet again before our eyes. We have entered the pre-teen stage. Gone are posters from Disney movies, rapidly replaced with the latest teen stars, Hannah Montana, The Jonas brothers, etc. As I father, I can best describe this as the eighth level of hell, but that is just me.

Sonya and I are more determined than ever that we want another child, yet now we have to have adult conversations to set realistic expectations. We decide that if it does not happen by the end of 2010 that we will be happy as is, with no regrets.

Our world changed, again...

In December 2008, our beloved Grandpa Snodgrass passed away at 98 years of age. We went off to the funeral home to see our entire family. While there, my mother introduced Sonya to Rachel, a long-time friend of the family. She was pushing a stroller with the cutest little girl. Rachel was fostering this child and most likely was going to adopt her. They talked; Sonya peppered Rachel with a million questions and was really excited about all of the information.

We had discussed foster care in the past, but we ruled it out based on the limited information we had. Our perception was that we would receive a child, and just as emotional bonds formed, that the child would be taken away from us. Those of you that really know me understand that I would be a wreck if that were the case.

Now, armed with all the new information that Sonya had learned, we decided to revisit this option. There we were, just like old times, riding around in the car with the radio off, having yet another famous discussion. We talked about all of the possibilities, have another baby of our own and understanding the risks, vs. fostering and taking on the risk of having a child removed from our home. We agreed that we needed to research foster care further, and Sonya took on this mission.

Over the next couple of weeks, she reached out to the center, a non-profit organization geared towards family services including foster care placement and adoption. We needed to discover what is "real" relating to this process. We found that you can become a licensed foster parent, while working with your own case worker to find the perfect placement for you. I was surprised that you can limit the placement according to age, sex, religious beliefs and other factors to ensure a comfortable fit for the child and family.

We agreed to go to Foster Care Orientation prior to making our final decision. Due to schedule conflicts we attended separate sessions. I walked into the center, thinking this is what I want to do; I want to help and maybe adopt a child. Over the next hour, I heard a lot of stories of how these children enter "the system." I also heard stories of how people get into foster care for the wrong reasons (namely looking for a state check). This killed me. Then I heard stories of how families were able to help children reunite with their parents, or transition into an adoptive family. I was exposed to legal requirements and the entire process.

I walked out of this room feeling that "THIS IS WHAT I HAVE TO DO!" I have to ensure that at least one child is welcomed into a loving home. I only needed to know if Sonya felt the same way.

We agreed to wait and discuss all of this over the weekend, while Tori was at Grandma's house (her preferred vacation destination), to allow us both time to process and read all of the provided materials. When we sat down to dinner Saturday night, we started talking and everything came out. We held back nothing about our hopes, dreams, concerns and fears. We agreed that fostering a child was right for us. Before we could go any further, we needed to discuss everything with Tori, as her life would be forever impacted as well.

When Tori came home on Sunday night, we sat down to discuss these dreams with our little girl. We asked her to take a couple of days to think about it and ask any and all questions she could think of. About ten minutes later, she said she wanted to be a Big Sister more than anything. We gave her a week and then revisited the topic. That talk did not go well. She was very upset that the process was taking too long, so yes, she was 'all-in' with us. At that point we had some fun decisions to make. When should we target this? What limits do we want to place on the placement?

Our plan...

Sonya had started school this past February to become a Registered Medical Assistant; I have been working full-time while finishing my degree. We have landed on September as our goal for getting our foster care license and being ready to accept a child into our home (Tori wants it all to happen faster).
Now we will start the process of obtaining our license and getting a social worker assigned to help guide us through this journey.

We have decided that we prefer the placement of an infant, whose parents have either signed away all rights, or have already been stripped of their rights by the court. We will all see how this works out..... In future posts, I will share the information discovered in the licensing process and will try keeping you updated, as we work through this.

2. Getting our ducks in a row... March 25, 2009 at 9:46pm

Armed with the plan - fostering an infant with the intent of adoption, and a September timeline - we think the hard part is over. Guess again! The guidelines for foster parenting (even though we want to adopt, we need to get the license first) include detailed rules for homes. Rules span from the minimum requirements of a bedroom, to rules about storing cleaning supplies. When you think about the importance and safety of children, these rules are needed. However, being a parent already (and yes, I think I am doing a good job), makes this all seem a little silly.

You may recall my mention of our dream house purchased last summer. Our 1800 sq ft ranch, resting on 2 ¾ acres in the country (a.k.a. heaven), is everything we wanted and then some. This house was custom built in 1979, and has three bedrooms on the main floor with an additional 800 sq ft of unfinished basement that just screams "Man Cave."

When we moved in we knew there was work to be done to this house to make it ours. The list includes finishing the master bath; creating one or two additional bedrooms in the basement, providing general upkeep, and applying fresh paint all around. Yes, we had taken on another labor of love. Pictures can be seen in my photo section.

We have made huge strides and turned the house into a home, yet we still have much to do, and the clock has started ticking. I have targeted the guest bedrooms in the basement to be completed in May or early June (I will delay the electrical work as long as I can) to make room for the baby's room. Speaking of the baby's room, the Boss has created a punch list of projects for it as well. It is going to be a lively spring. :)

Why are these home projects relevant? Part of the licensing process includes a home inspection along with interviews of family and references to ensure we are fit to welcome another child into our house. Despite the hassle, this is another step I fully support in the process. I am fully committed at this point; I have found my mission and accept it gladly. Sonya and Tori are ready to put in the work to make this dream a reality, so united we stand (how I love my family).

As strong as the three of us are together, we are not only changing our lives, but also the lives of our extended family and friends. Excited as the day we discovered Tori was coming to join us, we embark to tell everyone of our plan. I admit, I was a little nervous in some cases to see if everyone would welcome this child into the fold. My nervousness was quickly washed away in each conversation with a sense of pride as everyone thought our plan was wonderful. Assured with this support we continued to press on.

Being the "type-A", super-project-manager freak that I am, I plan out the home repairs prior to the inspection. Not everything on our list needs to be completed, but we need to prioritize organizing the bedrooms, creating the baby's room and child-proofing the house to get the coveted license.

During the month of February, we slow down. I focus on work and school while Sonya gets acclimated to her new school routine. I also took a much needed "guy's weekend" to allow me to recharge. Now back to work! I have picked up some additional lumber and will start swinging the hammer again real soon. Yahoo!!!!

Of course getting the house ready is only one thing we need to do in this process. We still have a lot of learning to explore in the foster-to-adoption process. We started PRIDE training on March 21 and it wraps up on the 28th (summary in the next post).

Thank you again for your support, I want to warn you the next post will cover some rough material as I review the PRIDE training sessions.

3. It's time to learn.... 3/29/10

Warning: This post is a tough one; this has been the hardest entry to write.

As you can tell from these posts, this journey has become a personal mission for us. We are dedicated to helping the center and their children any way we can. They will be forever in our hearts as we go forward, and already I feel that I am becoming a better person from this experience.

We discovered in orientation that to obtain a foster care license, we must attend a orientation class, receive twelve hours of training, agree to medical exams, undergo an interview process, and fill out a mountain of paper work. Our next step is training. Other than two six-hour sessions, I have no idea what we are walking into.

As Sonya and I are making the hour-plus drive this Saturday morning, I am feeling a little nervous. During the orientation, we will be exposed to stories of the children and families that enter "the system." When we arrive we are shown into a room with others who are going through the process as well.

We meet people with different goals; foster care only, others who wanted to adopt, and those who needed the license to care for relatives. With a common theme of helping children, the group is ready to begin our PRIDE training. PRIDE stands for Parents Resource for Information, Development and Education.

I can best describe this training as taking a drink from the firehouse (yes, a UHF reference). Information and personal experiences are shared at an alarming rate. Through reading, videos, and class discussions we cover both the positives and negatives associated with fostering children. Our instructor was very open and honest throughout the sessions, working to manage our expectations.

Please remember that the goal of this process is permanent placement for the child. This can be accomplished through either reunification or adoption.
The primary goal of foster care is reunification, where the birth family and child are reunited. This leverages foster caregivers (relatives or other family) to care for the child while the birth family gets things in order. In this scenario the birth parents still have a say in the way the child is raised. From hair style, types of food they eat, to religion, all of these decisions fall back to the guidelines of the birth parents. When the child is placed with the foster family, the foster parents work closely with the social worker and birth parents to ensure the child's needs are met.

Another type of permanent placement is adoption. If the parent loses all legal rights, the child is then placed into a pre-adoption family (this is us). During the pre-adoption period, legal and financial responsibilities are retained by the state. Assuming an adoption takes place, when finalized all legal and financial responsibilities of the child shift to the adoptive parents (often the child's last name is changed). Until finalized, the social worker and adoptive families work together to make decisions for the child.

All of this made total sense to me and I was like, "Yeah, we can do this." Then they started sharing real stories and videos that covered a variety of issues:

- Single parent gets laid off from work, gas and lights are turned off, and the kid is taken away to allow the parent time to get things in order.
- Children neglected due to parental drug abuse.
- Abuse (these stories have kept me up at night). Cigarette burns, broken bones and bruises. One case told of a child who was hit with a frying pan when asking for something to eat. Another case had a child placed into a tub of scalding hot water and then beaten.
- Then the one that broke me. Three siblings have been molested. They are taken from family but unable to prove the molestation in court. The parents still had weekly visitations with the children, while the parents were working to regain custody. My brain said, "Shut-up Tom," but I couldn't. I actually said out loud, "I don't know how open and supportive I could be with a birth parent, if molestation was involved." Our instructor simply said, "That is why it is good you are a pre-adoption family." Crisis diverted!!!

We also covered information around understanding the children's feelings during this process and how they may act out their emotions. The key to remember is that no matter what our perceptions may be of their past, their past is all they know. They will be desperate to return to it. These kids need support and stability, and when you are a foster parent, you will be forever joined to that child. You will become an anchor to help guide or support both the child and parent whenever needed.

We also discussed things I hadn't considered. For instance, we have discussed our desire of an infant (one year or less), and that was the only filter we agreed to put on our placement.

In our class we discussed cultural differences and personal needs of different ethnic backgrounds. They challenged us to research our community and see how the community would accept a multi-ethnic family. This point never crossed my mind. We knew race and ethnicity didn't matter to us or our family and friends, yet I didn't think of how our community would react. I plan on researching all of this, and I will report the results in future post. I don't foresee any issues; we will see what I find out.

We covered all of the services the center offers to assist the child and family in their ongoing needs. Then came the paperwork: an application, medical release forms for all three of us (requires a physical and TB test), police background checks and fingerprints, surveys for us and Tori, and more I am forgetting to list.

At the end of the second day of training, we left with our certificate of completion and many new friends that we hope to see again. We also have our checklist for what we need to do next:
- Complete and submit forms closer to September (when Sonya completes school)
- Finish all of our major house projects
- Setup the baby's room.

Setting up the baby's room requires getting clothes and diapers of all sizes to have when we get that much desired call!

We will continue to provide updates to let you know how things are tracking and keep you in the loop as we go. Thank you again for your support and well wishes. We will talk again soon…

4. Getting all of our ducks in a row... May 17, 2009

I know it has been a while since our last post, and we have a lot to catch you up on. When we last talked, Sonya and I had completed the required training. We decided that she would focus on school while I get the house ready for the pending licensing inspection.

As for now, she is rocking out on the honor roll, and I have kept up my workload and grades in school. As for the house, MAJOR progress has been made. The basement framing is complete. Insulation and over half of the drywall has been hung. As a bonus we removed the dreaded fire bush that was located at the corner of our house (45 ft in diameter and 6 feet tall - the darn thing had 30 stumps to be pulled out) and completed most of the demo in the master bathroom. These projects could not have been done without the help of our family and friends: Dad (there almost every step of the way), Tim (lent me his muscle and truck to kill the bush), my friend Eric and his son Ty (electrical – will be completed at the end of the month).

I was able to get my police fingerprints and physical out of the way for the license. Sonya and Tori (Tori only needs the physical since she is under 18 years old) will get theirs next month (after Tori has completed the school year). We are tracking a little ahead of schedule.

On another front, I brought my HR friend from work on a tour of the center. As a nonprofit organization they can always use some assistance. On the tour I learned that they offer many programs (besides foster care and adoption) geared towards the well-being of children. We saw a grief quilt created by children who had lost a loved one. We saw a beautiful mask painted by children with autism to illustrate how they feel. Then we visited the Magic Closet, where families can receive donated goods (food, clothing, or toys) when needed. I am working to get more information about the programs and will dedicate a whole post to just that in the coming weeks.

Again, I walked out of there with a renewed vigor about finding ways to help the cause. I will be volunteering some time and working with their strategy council to find other ways to help.

I wanted to take a minute to say thank you for all of your support. When Sonya and I started writing this diary, we never thought so many would take the time to read this and follow along. Our intention is to keep this and all of the feedback to share with the child when he or she is older, basically a way to highlight how excited we are for him/her to join our family. I have shared the previous post with our friends at the center, and they might be posting this on their page as well. We shall see where it all goes from here.

We will keep you posted as the license finalization process nears. September will be here before I know it.

5. Checking In ...Sunday, June 28, 2009

Based on feedback, we have gone too long since the last update.

Let's start with the basics. Tori finished 3rd grade (honor roll), Sonya is now a senior in her medical assisting program (honor roll), and I am down to my last year for my bachelor's in marketing (also on the honor roll). Lucy and Lily (dog and cat) could care less about any of that.

With Tori out of school, we needed to find child care while Sonya is in class. Our awesome neighbor introduced us to Cassie. Tori loves Cassie, and she is awesome. Did I mention how much we love living out here? Plus every other week, Tori goes to Grandma and Grandpa's to run her other kingdom. This kid has got it made.

Our family and friends continue to support us in every way possible (like reminding me about updates). We got the chance to go to a family function, a cousin graduated from high school. It was good to see everyone and catch up. Throughout the day we had aunts, uncles and cousins all express their support as we go through this process. I am very lucky to be a part of this family. Sonya's Mom and Dad finally got a chance to read all of these posts. I confess that I felt a bit odd sitting there while Dad was reading, but the love and pride he showed when he was done will be with me forever.

As for projects around the house: the basement is only twelve sheets of drywall away from being ready for mud and paint. The master shower demo is done, and I am waiting to replace the floor (this only gets worked on when there is nothing else to do and it's raining). Now that the weather is finally straight, we have shifted our focus to other critical projects.

Enter the living room! Sonya has painted the ceilings, and we are getting ready to prime and paint the walls. Painting will enable us to move the big-screen television upstairs to avoid all of the construction dust that will be in the basement. We will clean out the baby's room, and start painting in there.

While Sonya is busy painting, I have become "The Supreme Ruler of The Chainsaw," a title that I love. Tim came over and helped clean up another section of trees, leaving the two bad ones left to go. We also pulled out a lot of the dead bushes. All of this wood has to go somewhere, so we are burning it almost every weekend. I LOVE THIS PART!!!!

We have adjusted our plan a bit. We will have the entire upstairs complete and ready for the foster care inspection. We need to get the license prior to a child being placed with us. This will let me take my time with the basement, which is on hold till the fall (I prefer to play outside when I can).

Also, I will have a lot to do in the baby's room before the inspection. Of course we need to paint, but I also need to get the crib set up and ready. We need to buy clothes and diapers (all sizes, as we are not sure what child will come to us). Then Tori will want to pick up the critical toys that every child must have. She is really, really, excited.

We are still submitting our paperwork in September to get the license, and then it's left to a higher power.

I will try not to go so long for the next post, as the countdown clock continues to click.

See ya later, I have got to get back to work.

6. The countdown begins....Sept 4, 2009

So two months have passed since my last update, and things are still moving forward. Sonya finishes school on 9/4 and starts looking for a medical assistant job. Tori is getting ready to start the 4th grade, and wants to grow up way too fast. I am just 31 short credits away from being done with my degree. We got a new puppy. Tori named him Max (lab mix, almost 4 months old), and he and our beagle Lucy are best buds. Not to fear, our cat Lily is still the boss over all of them. It's like living with the Three Stooges. Never a dull moment!

We have made a lot of progress with our outside projects. We have cleaned four out of five of the wooded areas, and we still have a lot of burning to do. We enjoyed the pool this summer, and then put it away. We painted the living room and hallway.

Most importantly, we took a couple of weekends for us. We went to the company picnic, had friends over afterwards for a bonfire, and ate homemade chili. Then we invited the dreaded Moore sisters over with their families and had a BLAST!!!! Tori was able to play with all the kids, we pigged out, and I really liked the hubbies. We look forward to the next gathering.

Our plan is still to submit the paperwork for adoption at the beginning of October. We need to get some things ready for the pending inspection...

Now we are again shifting our focus on the inside of the house. I moved the TV and recliner up from the basement. We are scheduled for the 25th to complete the electrical, and I will start finishing the drywall the weekend after (YES!!!). But taking this approach has a cost. For the inspection which will most likely happen in October, we will not count the basement as livable space (until completed).

So this month is crunch time: We are going to paint and prep the baby's room (almost ready for the clothes that are hanging out there), prime and paint the kitchen and then get ready for the inspection and winter. I promise a post when we turn in the paperwork and to keep you updated.

See ya soon, Tom and Sonya

7. We are getting closer....Nov 3, 2009

Wow, things have really picked up in the last several weeks. The quick status on all of us: Sonya has completed school, passed the RMA exam and started working; Tori keeps growing (almost as tall as Sonya) and amazes me in new ways every day; I am back in school, after a few weeks off, and pushing forward and seeing the finish line. Max the puppy is the size of a small car and still wants to sit in your lap half the time, the other time he and Lucy hone their Ninja skills against each other (I am sure there is a master plan to take out the cat in the near future, LOL).

As for progress for the baby, yes we have much to report. We have painted the baby's room (light green, with white trim), submitted the paperwork to get the foster care license and been assigned a caseworker (more on this in a bit). We have also started loading up the baby's room. We still have a queen size bed in there until I get drywall done in the two spare rooms in the basement (slated for Dec, if things go right as life can get in the way sometimes). Also in the baby's room is a freshly painted dresser (white), and as of today, a baby crib (Tori's old crib). This is the first time we have had a crib in the house in almost nine years (I am the dad and allowed to get choked up here LOL). I am not sure how the room will be decorated, as we don't know the age or sex of the baby. Ok, we do know the baby will be one year or younger but that's it, I swear.

Our loving family and friends have been an incredible support system. We have been loaned a high chair, two car seats (different sizes), a stroller, and an ExcerSaucer (thank you Toni, Jeff and Aunt Kathy). My mother has been saving three garbage bags of clothes from a yard sale. After going through it, we found boys and girls clothes in sizes from newborn to 12 months. Now those clothes are all washed, sorted by size, and stored in the baby's room. Sonya and I went to a Mom-to-Mom sale (as a guy, it is just another type of garage sale with no tools). We got a playpen and baby monitor. We also have a supply of Playtex bottles (the ones with the plastic bags). We have received some warnings from others, that additional clothes are coming our way. THANK YOU EVERYONE!

So with a baby arsenal stocking the closets and baby's room, we now are on a mission to decide what we want to buy before the baby comes home (yes, I meant to say it that way). One thing is for sure, I will begin working to childproof the house, because we know how sneaky kids can be LOL.

As for the license, Sonya was told that we are getting a caseworker assigned. They will review all of our forms and complete an evaluation to make sure we are good candidates for a foster care license. I am not really stressing about this. We have passed the fingerprinting and police check, and it was a tad bit shaky there for a minute LOL.

When the caseworker has completed that process they will schedule the site inspection. This is the part I am nervous about, knowing that some of the projects have yet to be completed. We will have big wins with the baby's room setup and the childproofing of the upstairs prior to inspection. Also, we have to get Lucy (the beagle) one more booster shot prior to the license being issued.

We have no target date for the site visit, and we are at the mercy of the caseworker. Now I will not get upset at the caseworkers if this takes some time. They are really busy working with the kids every day, ensuring their safety, and placing them when needed. Along with teachers, I feel that social workers are drastically underappreciated. After the site inspection, and our license should be issued (it will be a 90 day temporary license, then the two-year license begins). Then we will be just waiting for a very special phone call!

I also have to say, I received a very good surprise regarding this process from my employer. I will be able to get paternity leave for a couple of weeks to assist in getting the baby and house adjusted after the phone call. That leave was not planned, but a very welcomed addition. This way I can hang out with the little one a bit too.

So there you have it. We are moving forward and things are starting to pick up speed. As always we will keep you posted.

Thanks Tom, Sonya and Tori.

8. Are we there yet???   November 29, 2009

When we turned in the paperwork three weeks ago, it was exciting and nerve racking all at the same time. Sonya, Tori and I are all really starting to realize that the baby is coming, we just don't know when. The last 25 days have been life as normal at the house. Tori and Sonya were fighting colds, Tori got her report card, and we are proud as always (we will be working to get that last grade up to an 'A' too). Sonya and I have been working and trying to keep things moving forward on the house. We actually started the childproofing process and have just a couple of cupboards left to go.

Then it happened! We got the call from our caseworker/licensing agent to come out for the house inspection. We scheduled it for the Wednesday before Thanksgiving to give me one additional weekend of prep time. We spent that weekend as any other, cleaning the house and catching up on laundry from the week. It seems to be our routine with everything that is going on during the week. With Sonya and I both working (she is loving the job, and is really happy with the atmosphere in the doctor's office), and Tori trucking through the 4th grade and Girl Scouts, we can tidy up during the week and then do the deep cleaning one day each weekend.

In addition to the normal chores, we had some really nice things happen too. I received a phone call from a dear friend that wanted to, "…Ask something, but I was not allowed to say 'No.'" Our friends Erika and Dawn are planning a baby shower of sorts for after the baby joins us. We are blessed with a wonderful family and friends, who are also gnawing at the bit for this baby to join us. This baby is going to be surrounded by love, just like Tori, and it is deeply moving to us.

The night before the inspection, knowing that I didn't have to work the next morning, I went to bed at the normal 11:00 p.m. time. I fell right to sleep and then woke up at 2 a.m., ready to paint the entire house. I might have been a little excited. So I got up and played video games, and did two days worth of homework. After Sonya got up and went to work, I was alone going stir crazy waiting for the caseworker to arrive (she wasn't due until noon), so I played more video games (yes, I am still a big kid and do not want to grow up).

When our caseworker arrived, I was one nervous person (not as bad waiting for the delivery of Tori, but it felt close). We walked room to room, measuring and surveying the area for safety. We reviewed the baby's room which has the crib and a queen-sized bed (until spring, when we finalize the guest rooms in the basement). She went into Tori's pink (I mean REALLY pink) bedroom and then the master. The entire time, I am explaining the different projects underway like the replacing of the master shower, and highlighting the plans if we have a baby in the house while working on it. She tested the water temp in the general bath (a.k.a. the airplane bathroom), we were a tad too hot (needs to be at 120 degrees max).

We continued through the kitchen, laundry room and lavatory. Then, as we were getting ready to enter the basement, I gave her a disclaimer about how the basement will not be treated as livable space until the projects are complete. I assume we will be done in March/April, and that includes installing the drywall, mudding, sanding, painting and putting in new carpet. She saw the framing for the three additional rooms (great room and two bedrooms). I had concerns she would not count one of the bedrooms, but the two doors (into great room, and adjoining door with other bedroom) met the requirements for it count. YES! Another win! She checked out the cold room and storage room (where the boiler and water heater are located).

After checking out the garage, we sat at the kitchen table to review her findings and to discuss my questions and the next steps. The change needed in the house for now was to lower the water temp (done). When we finish the rooms downstairs, she will come out again and update the profile. Shew! I had expected worse.

As for next steps, we started reviewing all of the paperwork we had put together and created the list that would be due for her next visit. This includes a financial statement, copies of birth certificates, shot records for the pets and our reference forms. I found out that she will be helping us by processing our request and write up for the license. Then when the license is approved and returned from Lansing, she may be assigned as our social worker or we may get someone else.

Then the interview started....
What do you want a boy or girl?
***Doesn't matter

Do you have any restrictions for the child?
***A year or younger and the parent has no legal rights.

Our caseworker let me know the restriction on parental rights could cause a longer wait for us to get a baby. She also said that there are so many kids out there that they are not able to process all of them. Some kids have to be sent to other agencies.

Now, I have worked in marketing for the last 13 years and am fully aware of what happened next. It's not a bait-n-switch, but most definitely an up-sell tactic that I agreed to. These questions made me consider some things I hadn't before.

What if we have twins? Are you open to take both?
***Mmmmm.. yes, (I'm thinking, how you can separate the two?)

What if they are mixed siblings?
*** huh?
Meaning we have an infant, but they have an older sibling, maybe a 3 or 5 years old.
*** Well, it is important that Tori remains the oldest. If there is an age gap of a couple of years, then yes. (I am thinking again, how can you separate the two?)

YEP, I may have just agreed to more than one. Just wait till Sonya finds out... LOL

Then we outlined the next steps. When our caseworker returns to the office on Monday, she will request a water inspection from Lansing (required, because we have well water). I will call her when we have the paperwork together to schedule the next visit. In this visit she will interview Sonya, Tori and me individually to assess how welcome the baby will be into our home. Then she will send her report off to Lansing, where they will review it, and then hopefully approve and issue us our license. TOO COOL!!!!!! About two hours after starting this process, she was off, and I had a Christmas list of stuff to find for our next visit.

The first item was how to tell Sonya about maybe getting a couple of kids. At 5:00 when she got home, I asked about her day (it was good) and told her how pretty she is. Her response: "What did you do?" So I explained the inspection room by room, and reminded her just how pretty she is (nope, didn't work that time either). Then I discussed the Q&A with the caseworker.

The one minor detail I left out earlier was that when I was talking to our social worker, and answered her questions, I blamed Sonya (LOL). For instance, "I don't know how Sonya will be able to say no to twins." I only tell you now, as I mentioned in the conversation to Sonya. "Oh sure, blame me," was her response, while laughing at me. She agreed with me, but didn't want me to blame her. She is an incredible person. She puts up with me and has a heart bigger than the moon. I am so lucky. All is well in the world.

We are wrapping up the paperwork today, and I am calling Monday to schedule the next appointment. As I mentioned, we are picking up speed. I am hoping we get our license soon, and then we will just be waiting for the phone call.

We promise to keep you updated.
Tom, Sonya and Tori ;-)

9. The Interview... December 23, 2009

Almost a month has passed since our last update, and things continue to pick up speed. The usual updates: Sonya, Tori and I are all doing well, working and doing the school thing. We have also been busy getting the house ready for the holidays. We would like to take a minute and thank all of you for your kind words, love and support through this process. We are blessed to have you as our family, and the new baby will be as well.

When we last talked we had just completed the site visit and passed. Yahoo! Sonya and I had to complete the additional paperwork, schedule the interview, and get the well/septic inspected. So we had it all setup for last Tuesday (12/15). Sonya and I had used vacation days, and the interview would start in time to allow Tori to attend the full school day. Oh, what a day it was.

As with most families, a day off can make you beg for a speedy return to work. This Tuesday was one of those days. It started with us getting up at 6 a.m., getting ready and dropping Tori off at latchkey at 8 a.m. Then off to Lapeer. Sonya is going to pick-up the Christmas lay-a-way (Tori can't find the presents at the store), while I go into The Home Depot to get the required items to finish the electrical work in the basement. A half hour later, Sonya pulls up in front of Home Depot, and we are off for the next leg of relay. We stop at another store and then hurry home for the water inspector's 10:30 am arrival. We had an hour to spare and used the time to wrap and hide all of the presents (success).

Because we are not connected to city water and sewage, the inspector has to check our septic field (to ensure it can support additional usage) and water for purity – what could be wrong? A call the day before primed me that we may need to dig up our septic field (several thousand dollars). If this is the case, our adoption goal would be on hold for a while. I was freaking out when the inspector showed up that morning.

We walked the house and yard while I answered questions. He took his water sample, taught me about my septic field and gave me homework. In order to be approved, I needed to dig out my wellhead (12 inches down and 5 inches around it). When we have some warmer weather, I need to re-route my drainage from the water softener to the outside and not the septic field. I had to have the digging done for the following Monday. Awesome! I already had a fully-scheduled week, and now I had to force this in.

After he left, we had an hour to go pick up something for Tori from the doctor's office before our caseworker showed up for the interview. We finally stopped to eat something, and were home waiting with a nervous energy for her to arrive. When she did arrive, we went right into the kitchen and started the conversation. That's what it was actually, not an interview but a conversation.

We discussed a range of topics from our life plans, employment history/plans, how we met and everything else under the sun. In what seemed to be ten minutes, an hour passed and Tori was at the front door returning from her taxing day in the fourth grade. The temperature was in the low 30's, and the kid "forgot" her coat at school (let's say, she was a bit excited about the interview). So we called the school, and I went to retrieve the coat, leaving Tori and Sonya to face the firing squad (LOL it was not like that at all). When I returned home the three were laughing at the table, and all seemed well.

So the conversation continued, and Tori started acting like a kid (hyper due to boredom). I asked her to go to her room while we finished. It took me 20 minutes to realize that was her plan the entire time (the little creep, LOL); she wanted to watch the rest of Twilight. After realizing my mistake, I went through her book bag and found my version of 'the golden ticket,' homework! So being the mean dad that I am, I made her come into the kitchen and join us. She had to complete her math work while we were finishing the interview.

Within the mountain of paperwork is a form that asks you about your thoughts towards parenting and your spouse. She read these out loud in front of Sonya. So every comment of mine that she read (usually followed by the, 'awwww'), made Sonya smile- which means, I had to deny it, in a feeble attempt to keep my man card. While this conversation was happening the caseworker got to see how we act as parents; while one of us answered her questions, the other would keep Tori focused on homework.

The interview lasted about four hours. At the end of it we received the nicest comment from our caseworker. She told us how much she enjoyed talking with Tori, and that we should be proud. She had what she needed to complete her report, except for the water and septic approval. As she pulled out, we made the call to order pizza (not a normal deal for us). I never thought the interview would last that long, but it was an easy process. We feel really good about it.

Now, back to that wellhead, as I mentioned we were booked solid for the weekend and the inspector is coming back on Monday. So Wednesday night after work, I was out there with a flood light, an axe (to break the frozen ground) and a shovel digging out the wellhead. My knee does not like the cold air, and really did not like kicking the shovel. But I am a man on a mission, and I got the digging done before Sonya got home. I was unable to kneel (too much pain) to remove all of the loose dirt. I was also given an early Christmas present; I had to cut through several tree roots, to clear the area. Yes, I am bitter. We got the rest of the dirt cleaned out Sunday; it took me a while to recoup.

Fast forward to Tuesday (12/22), the wellhead passed the inspection for the dig. We are waiting for them to release the water sample results. The report should be filed with Lansing the first week in January, and then we get our license. YES!!!!!!! From that moment (when the license is approved), we will be assigned another caseworker to assist in placing a child, and our name goes into the system.

To sum it up, the baby watch will start around Jan 15, 2010. Any time after that we can get the call. I AM SOOOO EXCITED!!!!!!!

When we receive the license, Sonya and I have to each complete another six hours of training within six months to keep it current. We can attend workshops at the center or other approved external sources - our caseworker will help us track this.

We are on the cusp of ending this leg of our great journey, and I need your input. Should I keep this log going through the placement and up to the adoption of the baby? Or should I stop here? Remember, this is going to be a bound book for the baby when he or she gets older, and all of your comments will be included.

Well that is all for now, have a happy and safe holiday. I am going to finish the drywall in the basement for Christmas (well the 2 days after). Then start mudding and painting. It will be a good time.

See ya soon,
Tom

10. Goodbye and Thank You!   December 31, 2009

Welcome to one of my deepest and darkest secrets. Several dear friends have said, "I don't know how you do it, dealing with the pain and pushing forward." Well this is one of the ways. Shortly after getting hurt, that wonderful day (I mean it), I started writing open letters that would never be delivered or seen by anyone. I would throw them away, burn them or just delete from the computer. These letters became a form of therapy, allowing me to say whatever was on my mind and giving me a small sense of closure. I don't write as many now, but I still write one every New Year's Eve, and for some reason I have decided to keep this letter as a reminder of this magical time. Don't feel like you have to read this; it's just my way of dealing with the world. Yes, I am One Hot Mess. Tom

2009: You were one heck of a year. There were health scares, injuries, and other issues like the economy falling into the crapper, the job and housing markets also tanking quickly. Then you add in the war, terror, and all the news stories of family issues and tragedy - at times it could really weigh me down. But as they say, "Life is a series of choices," and so here are mine.

I say thank you 2009, you made me a better and stronger person. I was taught that the job, world, and material things do not define me. I DEFINE ME, and I choose to define myself as husband, father, son, brother, uncle and friend, with everything else not meaning a darn thing.

Husband:

My wife, (the woman that did really save my life in so many ways) my moral compass and my partner through everything, made me so very proud during this hard time. She started and finished school; she pushed me to consider adoption (making me a better person yet again) and has lifted me up, every time my knee or emotions start to buckle.

Father:
My daughter, or daily personal reminder that things are still good in this world, is my greatest accomplishment. This year of change really can be seen in her. Gone is the baby/little girl, replaced with a young lady that is honestly the kind of person I hoped she would be. Happy, compassionate, loving, supportive, playful and sincere, just to list a few of her wonderful qualities. Her excitement over the pending baby and the prospect of being a big sister fills my heart with pride and joy every day.

The new baby, not here in body yet, but rather in spirit. Researching adoption and realizing my little way of making the world a better place has allowed me to grow as a person in ways I never imagined. Thank you, dear child, for providing me another source of motivation to keep me moving on the really painful days. You, your new Mother and sister are really the reason I force myself to get out of bed every day.

Son:
This year, much like 2008, allowed me to get even closer to my mom and dad. Yes they are my parents and friends, but also people I want to hang out with. Thank you for your continued love and guidance during the good and bad times. I know I am a grumpy gus at times, but it is usually because I know you are right, but I am still not willing to admit it. This is just one way I am attempting to cling to my youth.

Brother and Friend:
My sister is one heck of a woman; a full-time wife, mother of four, and a full-time student. When you and Archie took in 'A' this year and helped her out in that tough spot, you moved me. Your children are growing into great people, and you two should be very proud. Archie, my sister could have not married a better man, and I am honored you are my brother. I am so happy and proud of you and am thankful for our talks and Facebook fights (yes, I am taking the darn table). Keep going kid; I know you can tackle the world when you set your mind to it. Also, thank you for all of the great parenting tips and ideas, as I am sure I will still need them next year too.

For all of my adopted siblings, brothers and sisters from another mother, THANK YOU!!!! The love and support shown through the adoption post and every bump in the road, helps me understand that no matter what the world dishes out, love and laughter will always win. Although we may not be physically close as we would like, I choose to focus on the days together versus the others spent apart. Know that I am here for whatever, whenever you need it. This covers the full range, from a hug to a kick in the butt (just as you are for me).

Uncle:
I look at ALL (adopted and blood) my nieces and nephews, and see a bright future for the world. I see future leaders that also happen to be quality people. I saw one get married this year (darn that was tough), but I look at you all with a sense of pride and love. Growing up I didn't want to be called "Uncle Tom," now it makes me swell up with pride and God help the person that ever tries to hurt one of them.

This is how I want to be seen and what I see. I needed this year to teach me this valuable lesson.

As I look forward to 2010, I see a lot opportunity and good things.

My daughter will be ten years old, my wife and I will celebrate twelve years together, my parents will get to come to my house to visit and not work the whole weekend (maybe LOL), we will have a NEW baby in the family, and I will finally get my degree. I plan to get down to 250 lbs. and be smoke-free by the next New Year's Eve, and I will be surrounded once again by love and lifted when I start to fall.

Goodbye 2009, and thank you! Come on 2010!

11. What about now? February 15, 2010

It has been a month and a half since the last post, sorry for the delay. Life continues to move faster than I would like it too. Tori is doing well with school and Girl Scouts, but this pre-teen thing is an interesting show. Makes me want to apologize to mom and dad! Tori is a really good kid, trying to figure out if she is the kid or teen. I bet it's really confusing for her. On the upshot, she still likes to discuss her feelings and concerns with me or Sonya, so we are lucky and she knows she is not alone.

Sonya lost her job to the economy, and shortly after her van broke down for the last time. So we now are the proud owners of a 2005 Chevy Malibu Maxx, and we love the car. She has filled her days looking for work and getting the house ready for the baby. In the end, it was a good thing, as the office she was at was not a good fit.

As for me, well I spent January working on work, school and the basement. At the end of March all of the mudding, sanding and priming will be done. Thanks to Eric, the electrical is done as well. We were finally able to have a party with 30 people coming over for a lot fun and laughs and me being proud to show off the work.

Some big progress was made on the baby front too. When we last spoke we were waiting on some paperwork to be completed. That is all done. In fact last week, I received an email from our caseworker confirming that everything has been shipped off to Lansing. I confess this made me tear up. This week we should receive our license in the mail, and then it's waiting on the important phone call.

Having this time has allowed for some reflection too. I cannot thank all of you enough for your support, and reminders to provide updates. This blog started as an information tool for five of our friends that wanted details on the process. It has grown into so much more, and the outpouring of support and positive energy has been outstanding. I have been sharing these posts with our friends at the center, who have in turn shared the posts with other agencies within the state, and the impact continues to grow. I promise I will keep the posts going at least until the adoption is final, in the hopes we answer some questions for someone who is considering foster-to-adoption and may be unsure of the process like Sonya and I were.

One last very selfish thing as we get this license in the mail, LET THE BABY WATCH BEGIN. I know I am driving Sonya nuts, but it's like a long distance labor, just waiting for the call. I am going to be a Daddy again! How freaking awesome is that? Just wait until I post baby pics - you won't be able to shut me up.

Tom

12. Still Waiting... A time to reflect 2/28/10

First, thank you for following us to our new location. Your love and support has forever changed us for the better.

As for the blog, crazy I know, yet needed.

We have had a few requests from people who wanted to share our story with others they know. I say, "Yes, please do!" The downside has been that in order for people to see our updates, they had to be on Facebook and be my friend. So in the past I would email the posts to 50 people in addition to the FB notifications, and it was all getting too big to manage.

Then I had a chance to catch up with a dear friend, and she is really into blogging. After a few hours of laughs (yes, my sides still hurt), I started kicking around the idea about a real blog. Thanks to pain, that night I had time to put together this site. Please continue to comment. All new comments will be added to the old when we create the book for the baby. Also, the center is looking to get our story out to a larger audience, so we will see what happens and if the new format helps them.

With the new format, I will try to update weekly as things change. When the baby gets here we will have a lot of special steps to go through which are needed under foster care. Plus, I will have a lot of great new baby stories to share. Due to the fact that the baby is not ours until the adoption is complete, I may not be able to post pics - I am working to find this out. It's a small price to pay to have another little one to love, if that is the case.

Again, please feel free to share this link with anyone that may be interested.

Where is that license?????

Well the week has passed and the mail carrier did not bring our license. This is not a bad sign, but I am going nuts with anticipation waiting for it, and the call. We have had plenty to keep busy. I did a personal gravity experiment on Monday. I slammed my head into the wall and gave myself a slight concussion. Note to self, let's do that again never, yet the birds that came to visit me right after the fall were lovely. LOL.

Tori's birthday party was fun; all of the kids seemed to enjoy it. She had a blast and is getting back to normal from her sprained knee. She is such a trooper. Tori had to work the cookie booth this past Friday, and Sonya and I both helped. Yep, that's right, I am a Girl Scout. I was mad when told because I am an 'adult' I won't get my cookie badge. But to be fair, I am not sure I sold enough cookies to get it.

Sonya has been running all over the place for all of these activities. This week will allow us to get back into the normal routine. Even with all of these plans, Sonya and I both are going nuts waiting for the mail to arrive. I knew we wanted another baby, but I just didn't realize how badly. I actually teared up knowing the paperwork was in the hands of Lansing.

Here we are, still waiting on that piece of paper and the call that will follow. I know this could take a while, but I can't help from getting really, really excited. Thank goodness I have a lot of projects going to help distract me. Today I am playing with drywall mud again, while listening to the race.

Sending our love to Grandma, here is to a speedy recovery.

Hope you all have a good week.

Tom, So and Tori.

13. Really?   3/4/2010

Many of you know just how much I credit the center for making me a better person. Walking into those doors, I found compassion and was motivated to help at all costs. Sonya and I are adopting for what I can best describe as selfish reasons; we want another child to be forever with us. I created this blog to help our friends understand the effort and commitment required to foster/adopt. But no, that is not enough. I now also volunteer, with their Child Welfare Committee (CWC), trying to build awareness of the great work being done, and reminding everyone that there is yet more to do.

"Yeah, great Tom, but what about your license? Nope, it is still not here... We check the mailbox everyday hoping to find it, yet no luck. I know it is unfair to expect it so soon. But too bad, I really want it to get here. As each day passes, doubt starts creeping in, and we wonder if we will be approved or not. This is very nerve-racking... So we will wait and see.

While starting to lose the fight to self-doubt, the universe provided me a reminder of why this cause is so very near and dear to my heart. We had another meeting of the Child Welfare Committee, preparing for May.... What happens in May? You ask... stay tuned.

During this meeting with this group of compassionate people, all with a common goal of assisting families when they need help the most, my mission was renewed. Don't get me wrong, it's not like the doubt was pushing me away from it. But another log was definitely thrown on the fire.

You will notice that I mentioned helping families. Bobby, a dear friend that has been working with us from the center, reminded me of that point during a great conversation a couple of weeks ago. The goal of foster care is reuniting the family, arming both the parents and children with the tools needed to succeed. Only in the extreme cases is permanent placement needed. I can also tell you after my tour of the campus, they have some unbelievable programs to help the entire family in many ways.

While on this journey you will hear stories that will forever change you. Like some of the stories of how children enter the system (covered in an earlier posting). Today, I discovered more information with staying power. I know me, and I have conditioned my brain to process information in sound bites; here are some I heard of for the first time today.

From Fostercare.org
- "Currently, nearly half a million children in the United States are in foster care because their own families are in crisis and unable to provide for their essential well-being."
- "In addition, there are an estimated 12 million alumni of foster care in the U.S. representing all walks of life."

To bring this point home even further....
- In Michigan alone, over 18,000 children are in foster care right now
- Over half of Michigan's foster kids are from Wayne County

These four bullets will stick with me for a very long time. They helped drive home for me the magnitude of what is going on around me. I will also use them to help drive me to push forward. Yes, I am still selfish; I still want my baby to come home real soon. But I want to help the other families too. God knows it is nice to know that help is there if I need it.

I promise to let you know when the license comes…
Tom

14. Ok, I am going nuts..... 3/12

So we have spent another week waiting, and still no license! The self-doubt seems to mount more every day. So to distract myself, I decided to resume demo work on the shower in the master bathroom. Just two hours into it, I sliced (small cut, really) my arm on a loose piece of grout. Twenty minutes later I was in urgent care getting taken care of, or so I thought. Let's just say today, after my third trip to the doctor, we now have super-strong antibiotics to clear up the infection.

As for Sonya, I am sure I am driving her nuts calling everyday and seeing if the license has arrived. But she should be used to me now, or I would hope so anyway. We continue to work together to make the house ready and laugh with Tori every day.
Speaking of Tori... Let me start by saying that being a parent of such a wonderful child is the single greatest thing I have ever done. However, (you knew this was coming) somebody could have given me a clue about this pre-teen drama and demon transformation that is underway. Wow, I fear the stage of hating me is right around the corner. So it goes, she will grow out of it LOL. Maybe our caseworker was right. Maybe a baby boy would be good to balance the house a little. Right now it's me and Max (one of our dogs), and I am not sure that he would side with me if push came to shove.

Due to my infection I don't have much more to report, other than me going insane waiting. I will be making some updates to the site to include more information on the process as a whole.

As always, thank you for taking the time to join us on this journey and I will keep you updated as things continue to change.

Tom and Sonya

15. Another week down... 3/14/10

Well another week and still no license. Darn. Thanks to two more trips to the doctor. My arm is healing nicely, and I am starting to feel human again. Thanks to those that sent well wishes. It means a lot.

There seem to be little daily reminders that good things are coming. We are keeping busy and distracted as much as possible. A couple of our friends just had their first child (he is so cute) and through Facebook, I am reliving when we brought Tori home for the first time. Then my mind turns to doing it all over again, and I get really excited.

Last night during one of our regular family talks (we started these discussions a long time ago as a way for Tori to ask us anything and vice versa) it hit me. Tori started talking about when the baby gets here, and announced how much she wants it to happen. Sonya quickly followed with, "Me too, and I think Daddy is." (The best word in the English language is 'Daddy,' just so you know). The last 3-4 weeks, I have been so worried about this license; I didn't even realize it was driving my girls crazy too. So there you have it, all three of us are basically pacing waiting for the mailman to drop off the license.

I did have one more crazy idea.... Monday is Sonya's birthday. How cool would it be for the license to come as a gift for the whole family then? Yes, I know I am still rushing it, but I have to be me.

See ya again soon,
Tom and Sonya

16. WHAT THE H*LL? 3/20/10

WARNING: THESE ARE MY FEELINGS ONLY. This post is not a normal update; I am not out to share our experience within this post. Rather, I am getting this off my chest and needed an outlet. I promise the next update will be the normal sharing. I am emotionally charged on this one!

FYI – Still no license yet.
If you are new to following this blog, please see the archive to get the full story. For those of you that have been walking this path with us, I hope you continue, and that you are here to rejoice when the baby comes home. As you know, the day of our first foster care training session changed me. I found my purpose. This blog was started to answer all of the questions of five dear friends, and which I shared through Facebook. Now the plan is to create a book for the baby to highlight how important he/she is prior to joining the family.

I thought it would be a great idea to find out some facts and figures about foster care for my blog (scroll down to see them). Before I start this brewing rant, I want to say thank you to Paula and Bobby for helping me find these details.

Buckle up, this could get bumpy...
I am a 37-year-old loving husband, father, uncle and friend. I am trying to bring my daughter up to be a person I would WANT to hang out with, and it's working so far. We want another child so badly that I will happily jump through all of these required hoops, and be willing to do more. Yet, the following has rocked me to my core:

- Over 510,000 children are in foster care in the U.S. – the average age is 10
- The average length of stay for all children currently in foster care is 2.4 years

- 16% of the children in foster care have been in foster care more than 3 years
- Over 51,000 children are adopted annually from the foster care system.

These numbers are jaw-dropping, but remember, these families are getting help that they need. Most of the foster parents care only about helping that family through a rough spot.

As I mentioned in a previous post, horror stories discussed during the training taught us about how kids enter the system. These stories still turn me inside out when I think about them.

Then there are the stories of foster parents in for all the wrong reasons, using the assistance money as a source of income, neglecting or abusing the children.

Then I hear several news stories that ripped my heart out, time and time again. I sit here boiling with emotion, trying to make sense of it all:

- Baby beaten to death and buried in a hole in the backyard
- 7-year-old boy dies at hands of foster parents, after numerous warnings to child protective services
- 15-year-old girl impregnated twice, by biological father
- 4-year-old beaten to death by foster parents
- And there are too many more stories like these.

For the life of me, I cannot get my arms around this horror, and I AM SO DISAPPOINTED IN MYSELF for not knowing any of this until now. I know we live in a far from perfect world, and things are not all roses and rainbows. But, MAN THIS IS TOO MUCH. I would gladly cut off my arm for one of those kids.

Yes, I get it. Times are hard, the economy tanked, the job market is sluggish, and people need a helping hand. We all should help when we can. To me, nothing is more sacred and pure in the world than a child.
Bottom Line: I AM NOT GOING TO TAKE IT ANYMORE!
- I SWEAR to report anyone that is abusing a child
- I PLEDGE to help
- I PROMISE to give my time and heart.

Our neighbors need our help. These families have very little, and your love and support will go a long, long way to lift them up. I know that not everyone can foster a child, and I am in that group (see previous post). Good thing there are many other ways to help:
- Donate your time
- Donate clothes
- Donate school supplies
- Hold a coat, toy or food drive.

If you agree with any of these ideas, please share them with those that are close to you.
Please share your thoughts as I have done and leave a comment. Let me know what you think. Agree? I think I am just too close to this, and need to step back for a minute.
In the words of Billie Holiday and Arthur Herzog Jr., "God bless the child." Thank you again for your time.
Tom

17. Guess What........3/28

Well, another week down and still no license, but I am not upset. I understand licensing takes a while. But 4-8 weeks for a response, is like waiting on the cable company, "They will be there sometime between now, and the end of days." LOL

Last week's update left me with an emotional charge that resulted in me doubling my efforts to help out, while waiting for our baby. After finding and reviewing the numbers, along with the realization that each number is a young life that needs help, I was hurting. I was depressed. Then you changed it! I know it touched some of you too. Many of you have asked who to contact, what to do, offered support, or just echoed my feelings. For that compassion and desire to help, I say "thank you" on behalf of all of those involved in the foster care system.

This week also provided many conversations with great people whom I discovered have either adopted from afar or have fostered. I heard of one family that has fostered over 130 kids. I stop and look around at my world and see people with multiple kids and get amazed at their organizational skills. We will see how we do very soon. My sister and her husband have four kids. Just watching them is a testament to how fun and crazy a big family can be at times. I can't wait for our new baby. You can see shows where they have eight or ten kids – heck, teachers have to wrangle thirty kids at a time, sometimes more! Hats off to all of you!

Right now, Sonya and I are focused on a baby. We want to adopt an infant. Most of my posts to date have focused on children within the system. However, I am sad to say there are other demographics we should all be aware of. With that in mind, I wanted to take a minute and discuss the "age out" process.

Watch this 30 second video, Aging Out of Foster Care....Footsteps to the Future
http://www.youtube.com/watch?v=4oRFbw-MzGo

When a foster care child turns 18, he or she ages out of the program. Legally kids at eighteen are considered to be adults and are sent out into the world to fend for themselves. In a 2008 study of aged-out children from the Midwest, some equally stunning numbers were reported. To see the entire study follow this link:

- These children are twice as likely to NOT have a high school diploma or GED
- They are 14 times LESS likely to graduate from college
- More than 18% have been homeless at least twice in their adult lives
- 25% have experienced post-traumatic stress
- 72% surveyed have worked for pay in the year prior to the survey (with most making under $9.00 an hour)
- "The population of youth who are aging out of the foster care system each year is on a steady rise. These young people face many challenges which could potentially derail their successful transition to adulthood. Unemployment, poor educational outcomes, homelessness, and inadequate healthcare are all barriers to success. Moreover, youth are at risk for many negative outcomes that could affect their well-being..."

Just like the little ones, these foster care teens need help. The good news is that there are many ways to help in addition to becoming a foster parent.
- Donate your time
- Become a mentor

- Support education – donate school supplies, offer to tutor
- Provide transportation – many of these kids do not have cars, while many cities are reducing public transportation to balancing budgets

After researching this component of foster care, again my perspective has changed. I am now equally concerned for the older kids as the younger ones. Any parents or parental supporters, meaning those involved in the development of the child, take a bow! This includes teachers, aunts / uncles, extended families, and every adult in that circle of influence for a child.
We have a tremendous responsibility to help craft and lead our children into the world, positioning them for success.

If left alone, we see just how hard the foster care teen has to struggle. So, how do we as a community help those without parents or a parental support group? I, for one, need to find a way to help. This post is a start, but I will find another way. I promise you that.

18. No news..... 4/3/10

Another week down and we have to be getting close now; at least, that is the way I am going to look at it. We will continue to check the mail box daily. When the license comes, you will never shut me up. This past week was eventful in nothing but good ways. We had some high winds this weekend that snapped one of our 50 foot spruce trees and damaged our roof. We will call our insurer Monday and see how that works out. We spent the entire weekend just hanging out together and even had a bonfire. It is so nice to take a couple of days and spend time with my girls. I am truly blessed.

We also had a special moment that I must share. Tori received two rosebushes for Easter this year. According to her, these bushes are "the best gift ever." She then told Sonya that she knew exactly where she wanted to plant them, in the front of the house by her bedroom window (also close to the window for the baby's room). She looked at Sonya and said she wanted to plant one for her and the other for the baby. That little girl is so sweet and got us both to tear up with pride. She is 10 going on 30 with a heart of gold. I love her so much and would move heaven and earth for her if needed.

May is foster care awareness month. I have been working closely with a great group of people at the center to plan a few activities, so please stay tuned. One event that really excites me is the monthly birthday party. The center has a party held for all the kids celebrating a birthday that month. On May 1st Sonya, Tori, and I, along with some dear friends (Tim, Erika and maybe Tracy) will be there to make sure it's a special day. Just a few short hours of our time will generate a lot of smiles and laughter. Is it just me, or is a child's laughter the most incredible thing? I live to make Tori giggle, and it always warms my heart.

If I may be so bold, I am hoping you will help with foster care awareness too. Can you find a way to help make people aware of the foster care need? How you may ask? Use your Facebook status to share information. If you want to, feel free to share our blog with someone that may find it interesting (we are doing this to help others understand).

Spreading awareness is important for so many reasons. First and foremost there are kids and families who need love and support. We also have to educate people about this need and process. Sonya and I recently watched a movie called, "The Orphan." This story is about an adopted child who is portrayed as a trouble-making outsider. What a load of crap! Hollywood was out to make a buck, plain and simple. This horror and suspense movie is playing on a topic that many people do not understand, and turning that topic into a source of confusion and fear. People need to remember this is the same type of entertainment that tells us of a huge man in a hockey mask with a slight grudge against people, with a fondness for the outdoors. We teach our kids that television is pretend. Now we need to teach the adults too.

I hope to have news of a license soon and promise to let you know when. Thank you again for taking the time to read this.

We will see you soon.

Tom and Sonya.

19. Still No News.... 4/13/10

Another week down, and still no license. We should be no more than 2-3 weeks away. From my perspective, time has slid to a total crawl. I feel bad for Sonya. I call every day and make her check the mail, because I am not able to do so from the office. To be totally honest, yes I am frustrated and ready to scream.

As I have stated in the past, I agree that a careful licensing process for foster care parents is needed. However, I could have had my total portion of the license requirement done within a month or two. If we were not trying to line up the timing of getting our license with Sonya's last day of school, I could have submitted the paperwork months ago. Now that it has been submitted the state is taking forever (reality 4-8 weeks, seems like a year to me). I could have submitted the request while Sonya was still in school and not have all of this waiting now. Yes, I am grumpy and venting.

I know the following is true of me: I am a loving husband, son, father, brother and friend. I also know that I HAVE NO PATIENCE for waiting. This whole process of waiting on this piece of paper has only confirmed that issue. I am ready to drive to Lansing, sit on a desk like a paperweight, just pissing and moaning until I get the license. But I will not. As a friend of mine says, "One step closer to maturity!"

The following is most likely TMI, but a part of this story. This is your warning, read on at your own risk.

I am a project manager at heart. I plan to create a plan; I then manage against the plan, while developing the next plan. Type-A to nth degree!! I can joke about it, but I know deep down that it is part of me, for better or worse. Back in the day, while discussing this with Sonya, I made the following point, "When we get our license, one of us needs to ensure we will not get pregnant."

You may ask, why? We thought you wanted another child, and yes we do! More than words can say. But many factors came into play:

1. Twins run in both families. So if it happened as predicted, we would get the baby and then become pregnant with a litter. Yep, I was and still am, scared at the thought of three at the same time. It would be like a baby gang chasing me down with crap-filled diapers. I'm just saying....

2. I was also scared at the risk of another miscarriage. We have moved on from the last one; however, I would be lying if I didn't admit to freaking out every month we took a test.

3. Then, after training and hearing about the kids in need, I wanted to ensure that if we ever wanted more we would be forced to explore foster and adoption again.

I believe God has a sense of humor, as I review this logic. I was afraid of a litter and am planning on one (or more) now, and then even more as Tori and the baby get older. But I had a plan, and I was committed to following it. Being the manly-man that I am, I volunteered to get the procedure done.

So just about two weeks ago, I laid on the table talking to the doctor while he was playing in the most sensitive of areas with really sharp objects. What was I thinking? Hindsight is 20/20, and this was easily one of the dumbest ideas I have ever had. This includes the wonderful moment I pulled an all-night party the night before a final exam (Oh yeah, I failed). After this procedure I spent the better part of a week packing the tender area in ice (2 bags of frozen vegetables at a time), and won't know if this worked for the next three months. Yep," I am so smart, S-M-R-T!" (Thank you, Homer Simpson).

I have many funny, laugh-out-loud, graphic stories about this, but I had better not share them here. In the meantime, Sonya has taken charge and is kicking butt getting more things done around the house, so progress is still being made. The one true highlight of this portion of our waiting period was spending a day with dear friends competing in a Road Rally (supporting the Relay for Life). We laughed and laughed while running all over the city to take photos that will haunt us when the kids get older.

I am now walking in both the American Heart Association's Heart Walk, and the 24 hour Relay for a Life (with Sonya) on the same day. I hope I won't need frozen veggies for that one. Tori is working hard on her Math-A-Thon for St. Jude's medical center (I have a darn good kid), and we are looking forward to the next road rally. Oh yeah, our plan for the baby: that license will come, just never fast enough for me.

We will see you soon.
Tom, Sonya and Tori

20. I feel like singing from the rooftops, because when it rains, it pours..... 4/21/10

Question: Why no updates?
Answer: No time and nothing to report.
That all changes RIGHT NOW! Keep your seatbelt fastened, because this is a very cool ride.

Last week a family incident required my mom and dad to go to Tennessee to see my grandmother. She decided to put her house up for sale and move back to Michigan. I had already been planning a trip to Tennessee to pick up a couple of things, thereby freeing up car space for this summer's family reunion. When she put her house on the market last Thursday, we were hoping to get her here over Memorial Day weekend.

You can imagine our surprise when she accepted an offer this past Sunday. Now we are in scramble mode, planning a fast trip down to help get ready for the pending move. My fun trip has now turned into work, as I will start packing. She will be living in Michigan as of the weekend of May 14th. I am having daily planning conversations with Mom and Dad as we try to figure out the best way to handle it all.

Then today the world was turned upside down in the best possible way. While in the middle of a meeting I received a phone call from our caseworker. Apparently our license had been closed in error, and she had been working to get the matter resolved. We should have the license in a week. WOW, we are getting so close.
Then I heard, "We also have a set of twins looking to be adopted." My heart jumped in my chest, my eyes filled with tears. "Tell me more," was all I could get out. "They are two years old, a boy and a girl. Would you be interested?"

The tears started to fall at this point, and I was in total shock. I spoke in what sounded like a foreign voice from afar, "Call Sonya and ask her, I am for it, but she needs to agree too." I gave the caseworker Sonya's phone number and said goodbye. The next twenty minutes seemed like three weeks, no call back at all. I couldn't take it anymore and called Sonya. She said, "No" when I asked if she talked to the caseworker. I explained everything to Sonya, and heard the joy and tears coming through my phone. We agreed that we wanted the twins.

Sonya was off to call back the caseworker. She could not connect. We agreed to both try until we got through. I called and went to voicemail, pressed 0 and then asked for her supervisor…. Voicemail again, I pressed 0 and then went to her boss. When he answered the phone, I quickly explained everything that happened and ask that he let them know that, "We don't want to lose these twins." He was off to let them know.

Crap, I had to get to my meeting, right after I got the waterworks to dry up.

Sonya called me twice while I was sitting at that table struggling to maintain my cool and focus on the topic at hand. Finally, like a gift from God, the meeting was over. I rushed out of the conference room and called Sonya.

We have learned the following information:
- When the license is in the system (a week to ten days), the kids will be placed with us
- We are trying to get a meeting with the kids prior to placement, so they will feel more comfortable when the placement occurs

- The kids are over the age of being able to share a room (because they are a boy and a girl)

We had stuff for one child, not two. The flurry of activity that has occurred since then has been amazing. The soon to be grandparents, aunts, uncles have all shed some tears, and our friends have rallied the troops to help get a second bed and double stroller. Some friends are already looking for clothes. Wow and thanks are all I can say (which will never be enough, but is all I have at the moment).

Tori is looking forward to sharing her room for a couple weeks while I finish her new room in the basement (Lord help me). I will get started with that project when I return from Tennessee. While I am gone, Sonya and Tori will be putting the finishing touches on the house and making the list of what we need to buy when I get back.

The happy tears are flowing again, and I am too excited to think straight. I will provide another update early next week as more information becomes available.

Thanks again,
Love Tom, Sonya and Tori

21. You say hello, I say ok, sure.... 4/29/10

Come on, what can happen in a week? A heck of a lot, that's for darn sure. I wish I had the answers to all of your questions, but I don't. Here is what I know

-One boy and one girl
-Age: two going on three years old
-Size 2t-3t but skinny
-They are African-American
-They are OUR KIDS

During the last week, I went to pick up Pete (four hours in the car), then went to Granny's (another eight hours), stayed for twenty hours in Tennessee, and then came back. The trip was fun and productive. Granny is moving back to Michigan from Tennessee within the next month. While I was away, Tori and Sonya had begun what can best be described as the nesting process. For those of you that have had children you understand this, for those that have not... Well, think of it like this – nothing is clean enough, nothing is in the right place, and you will not listen or rest until every last thing in the house has been moved no less than twenty times within two days.

I am so thankful they have been in this stage. I have been super busy at work with an important deadline and have not been of any real help in the prep work. But we have much left to do and this weekend is going to be fun. We are volunteering at the center on Saturday, and Sunday is dedicated to getting the basement child-ready again. Plus we need to run to the store to get personal-care items for the twins and do the grocery shopping.

Our amazing friends are planning a "Welcome to the Family / Third Birthday" party for the twins on June 5th. These kids are going to be surrounded by loved-ones and the party is shaping up to be a ton of fun. In the meantime, we need to do some research on hair care. We need to prepare the house. Plus, I need to get cracking on Tori's room. I must be forgetting something…. Oh yeah, any day that phone can ring, and the twins will be on their way. Yes, those of you that really know me are SOOOOO right. I am going insane waiting on this! I cannot wait to hold them in my arms and welcome them into the family.

I will end here for now; hopefully another update will follow really soon with the arrival details.
Thank you,
Tom, Sonya, and Tori

22. We are so close that it is killing me... 5/5/10

I have so much to cover in this one so hold on tight...
Still no twins in the house but the day is coming really soon.
The license will be finalized within the next couple of days,
and then we will be one wonderful day away from our new
family members joining us. Yes, this is driving me nuts! Thank
goodness I am buried at work, or I would really be screaming.
Plus, we had the Most Wonderful Thing happen to us (read on
for the details).

The rooms are ready. The twins are bringing some toys and
clothes with them, so we are not sure what we need to pick
up. We have finalized the dates for the welcome home / open
house / birthday party. Oh yeah, did I mention that our
wonderful case worker sent us pictures of our new boy and
girl? Yes she did! I can tell you they are beautiful and look
very happy. Some have said that the little boy has that same
trouble-making look in his smile that I have.

To you I say, "Darn Right! It works for me and will for him
too." LOL

I have to let you know that I CANNOT share pictures online
of the kids until after the adoption is finalized. This rule is to
respect their privacy while in the care of the state. When the
court allows them to be legally part of the family, then I will
share a few pics of the family in action.

So what was this Most Wonderful Thing? Saturday our friends Jill, Erika, and the girls, joined Sonya, Tori and me at the center's monthly birthday party. Every month they hold a birthday party for the kids in any of the programs (not only foster and adoption, there are over twenty unique programs) where the kids can invite family and friends to celebrate their birthday. We had a blast playing the games, giving the prizes, singing happy birthday and serving the cake and ice cream. For one day these kids that have had a rough go of life were able to smile, laugh, play and be kids. Many of these kids don't get to have a birthday party, for a lot of reasons. This day was special for them and us too.

Jill, Erika, Sonya and I were blown away by the wonderful emotions that day. The three girls were awesome helping and having fun the entire time. The guests of honor had a blast, and provided big smiles, thank you's and hugs when the event was all over. This was easily one of the best days I have had all year. If you get the chance, volunteer for the day. It will make you grow in ways you wouldn't believe. Like the Grinch, my heart grew three sizes that day.

We left the center better for being there, with a sense of motivation to return as often as we can. We have been discussing other ideas on how to help the children and have another excuse to spend time with them. Not sure why, but we all felt a pure joy there and are working to feel it again.

Well, hopefully the next post will be some drawn-out emotional speech about my kids coming home. I am getting a son and another daughter out of this deal! I WIN!

As always we will keep you updated.

Tom, Sonya and Tori

23. What a Day! Part 1: Stay Tuned..... 5/14/10

We still have heard no word from Lansing for the license. They are backed up and had to prioritize the license requests for relatives. That's when an aunt/uncle or grandparent is going to care for the child, and therefore that guardian needs to become licensed quickly. Work has been nuts, which is good news as it helps me forget about how long we have been waiting. When the fact about timing hits me, I confess I get a tad pissy. We want our kids to come home; we are waiting to properly celebrate Mother's Day with all of the kids.

Then add in the fact that we finally watched The Blind Side this past weekend. I recommend this movie for everyone. Oh Lord, yes there were tears, a feeling of pride, and a feeling of "hurry the heck up, already." We have each thought, but have dared not say, that we are scared. Part of us is scared that if this process takes too long, the kids will be placed with another family. But not to worry, we are covered – they are in fact our kids.

We have talked to our transition therapist a few times to develop a plan to make this step as easy as possible for the kids. We understand that both the therapist and the current foster parent have been discussing us with the twins so they have an idea of what is going on. The big news right now is that Sonya and I are supposed to meet them today. The current foster mom has agreed to meet us and the therapist to support all of us. I have never had the chance to meet the foster mom before, but am forever in her debt for doing this.

I sit here just a few hours away from meeting my kids for the first time. I am printing pictures so they can see their new big sister and pets, and can take the photos when they leave. I would be lying if I said I am not nervous, just not for the reasons you may think. I am worried that I will be emotionally destroyed having to leave them when the meeting is over. I can't explain it except to say, I can't wait for them to come home.

Times like this tend to make you pause and reflect. It has been one heck of a ride, but we wouldn't change a thing. We are so close and time stopped along the way, making days seem like months. But for one afternoon, we are going to hang out and start the process of getting to know these kids and earning their trust. I will provide an update later and let you know how things go.
Thank you again for your time.
Tom, Sonya and Tori

24. What a Day! Part 2: I see our future and I love it!!!! 05/14/10

As discussed, Sonya and I were able to meet the twins today. This happened by the good graces of the current foster care mother and the center. We had the location and time setup earlier this week and have been going nuts all week, waiting for today to get here.

I had no idea going into this meeting of what to expect. I was concerned that it was going to be horrible for me, having to leave them when it was over. I was not sure how to introduce myself to the kids. I was afraid the therapist would say we were not a good fit. Any bad idea I could come up with played through my head during the ride there. I arrived today at 1:10 pm and was the only one there. I went inside and found our representative from the center; she was wonderful by the way. We talked and I was able to find out more about the twins. Just a few short minutes later Sonya walked in, and we transported far away, sitting in an imaginary delivery waiting room waiting for our kids to arrive.

Then three beautiful kids entered our twins and their current foster sister, all being led into McDonald's by their foster mother. She was wonderful. I knew right away our kids were good, happy and healthy. I sat there trying not to tear up; I didn't want to freak out the kids after all. We all moved to a table in the back, introduced ourselves, and then it happened. Sonya was introduced as "Your Forever Mom" or "Mommy Sonya," and I was "Daddy Tom" or "Forever Dad." I welled up full of emotion and pride and have still not come down yet. We gave the kids the stuffed animals I picked up along the way (thank you Kelly for the idea) and the pictures of us and the family pets (and thank you Marla, this was a huge hit).

We spent the next two and a half hours getting to know everyone. We played peek-a-boo and I am convinced they won. We had McNuggets and French fries. We talked about the pictures and just hung out. The twins accepted us right away, allowing us to pick them up, giving hugs and kisses and melting our heart. These two have no clue how spoiled they will become, when all of you get a hold of them. I am the grown up, after all, and would never spoil a child.

They took turns wanting to roughhouse with Daddy, and I know for a fact that he LOVED it. Sonya had similar experiences during our party; yes a party - that is what our visit became. They live to giggle, which means Tori and I have two more joining us in our quest to drive Sonya nuts (she has no chance now). Speaking of laughs, they have the sweetest belly laughs, and for me there is no better sound. I still will do anything to get Tori to laugh like that. Tori was not able to make this visit because she had school. When we got home we showed her pictures and told her about her little brother calling her when looking at the pictures.

Time was up way too fast. We needed to get home in time for Tori getting off of the school bus. Hugs, gratitude, and love were shared all around. The kids gave us hugs and more kisses, you can never get enough of that, and we needed to leave. I had to thank both the center and their wonderful foster family for discussing us with the kids and letting them know how much their new family loves them and is waiting for them to come home. My fear of leaving them disappeared. I didn't want to leave them, but was able to leave knowing that they were loved, happy and cared for while we wait for Lansing. Next to Tori being born, or Sonya agreeing to marry me, this day ranks as one of the best in my life.

One other thing must be said. These two little angels have developed a joint operating agreement when testing the rules. They were such cute, typical two-year-old kids. You say don't go past that line, they then step on the line. Come back in a minute and step over it, then a few minutes later they bolt past it like they are crossing the finish line of a marathon. I had forgotten how fun that part was.

So I am here now several hours later, unable to return to Earth from this wonderful emotional orbit I have been in. I still see the smiles, hear the laughs and feel the hugs. I will sleep well tonight, knowing that they are excited too. We will get them home soon and then you will get to see what we saw today. Any concern I had of having different feelings for them vs. Tori is gone. They are all my kids. I am dedicated to loving and protecting all my kids and heaven help you if you get in the way. It is amazing how quickly parents lose all power when kids are around.

Thank you God, we are so blessed to have our friends, family and all of our kids. We will keep you updated, go hug your loved ones and have a great day.

Tom, Sonya and Tori

25. Another week down and..... 5/23/10

Well we are now one month from the wonderful phone call, asking us about the twins. I am sad to report they are not home yet. This is the fault of no person but rather, an overtaxed system that overloads people with cases loads the size of Mt. Everest. Every day has been trying, hoping that today the kids will come home, with 5 p.m. passing and disappointment kicking in. I actually am off school until June 6. I requested the time to spend with the family, but they are not all here.

With good things coming to those that wait, I have got some great times heading my way. I have been swamped at work and not really much help around the house. Sonya, Erika and Dawn are off and running planning the party that is scheduled in two weeks. Yes, we have plans in place to ensure the kids are here for the party, even if the state has not approved our license in time. This weekend has allowed me to start the prep work around the house as we get ready to welcome them home in style.

While I had a really late night at work, Sonya and Tori went to a foster care support meeting at the center and were able to spend time with the twins. Sonya owes you the update on that one (feel free to send her hate-mail on Facebook LOL). I was able to talk to them on the phone, and Sonya sent me the first pictures of my three kids together. I am truly blessed and thankful. Both Sonya and Tori have been on cloud nine, and Tori is even more pumped to be a big sister. She told me when the twins giggle it makes her feel tingles in her tummy. We will keep you updated as more information becomes available, but that is all for the moment.
Tom, Sonya and Tori

26. Our Version of Childbirth 5/25/10

From Conception to Labor = 12 years
That is how long it's been since we first discussed the option
of adoption. I can clearly see us on a date, sitting in my blue
Ford Ranger in the middle of an empty parking lot, discussing
our plans for the future. Within the last year we became ready
to actually make the adoption dream a reality. Then the
training, self-exploration, tears, the smiles and the love, that
followed. WOW, the love, the love and support we have
received and STILL are is amazing and frankly surprising.

Labor = 1 month plus
One month ago we entered labor with a simple phone call. We
were asked about twins and jumped at the chance. Then we
had thirty days of breathing, pushing and fear. Fear that
something would be wrong and that the license would be
refused. We had our first meeting with the twins, and the
world stopped that day for me. All that mattered then and
now is to get my entire family in my house and start the next
journey together. Then Tori got to meet her brother and sister
for the first time. I cannot describe her level of excitement. I
know she is going nuts (like Dad) just waiting. She is
constantly bringing the twins up in conversation and telling
me how excited she is. She will make a GREAT big sister.

We decided to delay celebrating Mother's Day until all the
kids were home. Sonya and I seem to take turns expressing
how much we want our kids to come home. It's funny how we
instinctively seem to take the opposites ends of the discussion
to support each other. She is one amazing woman, but that is
the last nice thing I can say about her (because I know she
reads this).

Now, the next stage = (who knows how long)

Yesterday we got the call! Lansing came through, and now we have our foster care license. I actually looked it up in the system today to confirm it was not just a dream. We have done it! We are at the next hurdle. The center is working to setup the required PPC meeting (I forgot what this stands for - cut me some slack we've had a couple of big days). This meeting will discuss the plans and placement for the children. When complete, we can then bring the kids home. To say I want this meeting to happen now would be kind of obvious, but I will say it anyway (in case they read this LOL).

Then our next steps will be to work with the twins' counselor to ensure a smooth transition into the family. We will also start working with our adoption caseworker to begin the next leg of the journey, legal adoption. Sonya has met with and says a lot of good things about our adoption caseworker. In the short term we are inviting the grandparents over for a bar-b-q for a proper introduction before the party. I am sure there will some good stories coming from that one.

I will say this as frustrating as this journey has been sometimes, this path as been a real growing experience. I am sure time stood still there for a while, but I have learned so much about myself and who I want to be from all of my conversations with you. Now I am like a dad-to-be, pacing in the waiting room just waiting for the arrival. I am thinking of the next few years and all the great things that will happen. So I smile and I tear up, but make no mistake I am happy, and I am ready for this ride to start.

Thank you again for your time,
Tom, Sonya and Tori

27. Just one more sleep..... 5/27/10

I will start this by say that this is my last post.

Ok, maybe just my last post before the kids comes home. As you know, this week we got the call and the prized license. We have a meeting tomorrow and the twins should be coming home with us. I'm not sure what the adoption process will be like, and now I don't care. I am bringing my babies home, and we can be a complete family now. Basically I am a six-year-old waiting for Christmas Eve to end, so I can get to those presents waiting under the tree.

This leads me to the following important messages:

Thank you, everyone for the support.

Thank you, to my team at work. I have been grumpy from time to time from waiting.

Thank you, to all of the caseworkers that helped. Nashae, Crystal, and Samantha, you all rock!

Two special people should get medals for dealing with me when I am an emotional wreck in the final waiting period.

Thank you, Gloria in Lansing for putting up with my daily phone calls and for your follow up calls.

Here is the plan for the next few days:

Friday, we will go to the meeting and bring the kids home. We will be at the center at 10 a.m. We will meet with the DHS rep, our caseworkers, the foster parents and the kids. We will discuss the placement of the children with us and get a bunch of details. Then we will come home. Sonya and I will introduce the kids to the house and the pets. When Tori gets home we will have a lot of family bonding time. Saturday will be full of more fun and bonding as a family. We have invited the grandparents (both sides) over so the kids can meet them. This process will repeat throughout the week as we near the birthday party.

I promise to provide you all the details that I can, but the next couple of days are reserved for us. I will provide brief updates after we tuck the kids in for the night.

28. The kids come home and all is right in the world. 5/28/10

I come to you now as a parent of three, a ten-year-old girl, and a set of two-year-old twins (a boy and girl), and I am darn proud to tell you all about it. All three of my kids are fast asleep in one bedroom having a pajama party; it is really just too cute for words. The last twelve hours leading to this moment have been a roller coaster of emotion that in total make a "top three" day of my life.

Today started on a great note. Tori, only minutes after waking up, declared today as "The Best Day of My Life." I asked why and she replied, "Because I am finally a big sister today."

We were due at the center at 10 a.m. for the PPC meeting. For those of you that live outside of Michigan, let me explain we have two seasons – winter and construction. Our state tree is a construction cone and the bottom line - don't plan on getting anywhere anytime soon. We left our house at 8:05 a.m., right after Tori jumped on the bus for what I am sure was a very non-productive day at school.

We pulled into the parking lot one half hour early and went inside to sign-in and wait in the lobby. Just a few minutes later the kids came in through the door with their foster parents. I have the utmost respect and love for these two. They took great care of the kids, and I hope to keep them involved in the kids' lives as they grow up. When our female twin saw me I heard, "DADDY!!" and she ran into my arms, followed quickly by her brother. Yep I cried, and am now too... I mean, I have dust in my eyes. Oh yeah, they had a similar reaction when they saw Sonya, but I am pretty sure I am the favorite.

We left the kids in the playground with their foster dad, while Sonya and I were shuffled into a room full of people. Some we knew, while others we did not. We spend the next hour and a half discussing everything about the kids, such as their back story, medical history, personalities, social interaction tendencies and every other aspect of their care you can think of. When all the discussion ended, we sat there waiting to hear if the placement would occur.

The representatives for The Department of Human Services, the center, the adoption, placement and ongoing caseworkers, and the therapist (the one constant person the kids have had in their life) all had to vote for us. I am proud to report, they all voted for us. This group of ten people gathered to discuss and decide what is best for the children. You could feel the pride and compassion in the room towards our kids, very refreshing indeed. It was confirmed that we cannot share pictures of the kids until the adoption is final, so if you come to the party I will take pictures and share after the adoption is complete.

With the vote over (8 for and 0 against), the kids were placed with us. We setup meetings with the therapist and adoption caseworker for next Friday. We need to complete our yearly clearance process again and take the kids for their dental checkup all within the next thirty days. We spent about a half hour hanging out with our extended family (foster parents and the kids care team) playing in the playground of the center. Then with hugs, kisses and more hugs we agreed it was time to go. We walked out to the car and transferred the kid's belongings into our car.

These two have been in the system most of their lives, and everything they owned came to us in two trash bags. Note that most foster parents have the clothes and community toys at their house so little seems to travel. They also had their stuffed owls that we gave them in our first meeting at McDonald's. We were told that the owls travel everywhere and sleep with them too. Yep, more dust in my eye. We made sure to invite everyone to the party. Then the family was loaded in the car and off we went, the four of us heading home for the first time.

At noon we decided to stop for lunch. We found a Coney Island and they each got chicken strips with fries and a fruit punch. They ate their food, part of my cheeseburger and loved the juice. The, "I love you's" flowed around that table like running water. I swear the smile they have when they tell you those three little words can move mountains. Tori has this same power. I am in deep trouble, but I love it.
On the way to Wal-Mart we had our first disagreement. Our son wanted us to sing the ABC's and his twin wanted the Itsy Bitsy Spider. In the spirit of democracy we sang both, along with Row, Row, Row Your Boat.

If you have read the past post, you know how moved I was when we celebrated the birthdays for all of the center's kids (for two months). Well, today was a series of amazing moments. .We went to Wal-Mart on a mission. We needed a children's music CD (I didn't think to put one in the car), and our kids needed some toys of their own. I took our daughter in one basket, Sonya took our son, and we were off. We got Dora, Elmo, Trucks, the CD, and other fun prizes. I seemed to get more dust in my eye while at the store when our daughter was hugging the box that held Dora; I am wrapped tightly around their little fingers already.

We got home with an hour to spare before Tori gets home for school. So we introduced Max, Lucy, and Lilly (2 dogs and a cat). They were a huge hit, kisses for all, giggles and other fun moments. We showed the kids their bedrooms. After a discussion they were to spend the first few nights sharing a room, like they have at their foster parent's house. The bus stopped in front of our house and out came Tori. When she got close to the house, the twins were standing on the couch and shouted out the window, "TORI!" They all hugged, Tori had a few tears pop up and then they started playing. At one point she was getting tackled by her brother while lying on the floor. She loved it! Kind of strange, as she is usually the one that attacks.

We loaded up into the car and were off to the store again, to buy some clothes and supplies for the introduction bar-b-q on Saturday with all the grandparents. Can you say "Spoil?" I predict a fun-filled Saturday. We left the store with new sandals; a couple of outfits, some new pj's and yes, a toy or two. When we got home the kids decided they wanted pizza. Then they brushed their teeth, took baths, got dressed (sort of, I will explain) and then chilled while watching Toy Story. Before you know, one passed out, then two, and a while later number three was fast asleep too. Just an all around awesome day!

Sorry this post was so long. Just remember I warned you that it will be hard to shut me up. Thank you again for all of the support and taking the time to read this.
Tom, Sonya, Tori, plus 2 :-)

29. More than I hoped for... 5/30

For the record, there is still a lot of dust in the air, but I am doing better. I hope it avoids your eyes too.

Just two days ago the kids came home. As they walked into the house I was nervous as to how they would adjust to their surroundings. This boy and girl seemed to feel at home in a matter of minutes. Now they own the whole place, almost. They haven't discovered the basement yet, but that will happen today after nap time.

I have so many little stories, but I will provide you some highlights of the last sixty hours. They have each petted, hugged and kissed the dogs and cat. They know that they can have movie time in their bedroom, and they will clean it up when asked (hope they teach the big sister this one, LOL). I can also tell you that bath time is the most wonderful time of the day. They take such joy in getting all slicked up in the tub and then streaking the house while we are trying to catch, dry and dress them. I still do not understand why "naked-time" is so cool, but they are fast, with wonderful giggles as they run from us.

Yesterday the kids got to meet their grandparents and one of their great-grannies. Houston, we have a problem! The twins turned on the charm and now own those people. Those kids were spoiled with toys, new clothes, playtime, hugs, kisses and a lot of laughs. The kids seemed to take turns wanting to be held by all the grandparents. Our new daughter was singing, and our son was talking and charming the grandmas. He is a little player, waving and flirting with the ladies. Next week will be fun to watch these two hold court.

They were also given a swing-set (thank you Aunt Teresa, Uncle Archie, Granny, Grandma and Papa) that is so much fun to put together (thank you Grandpa and Papa, you guys rock).The kids spent a lot of time playing on a Little Tykes slide and chasing down the target of the moment. Tori loves being a big sister, but did mention today she thought they needed a nap, as "they seem cranky." As bad as this sounds, that was a small win for me. I took the chance to let her know that is how she acts when she is sleepy.

I am happy to report the kids are eating well. For example, yesterday at dinner they each had 1 ½ hotdogs, a few bites of Grandma's cheeseburger, a few bites of Cole slaw and potato salad. Then about an hour later, they had a piece of the welcome home cake from Grandma and Papa. They tended to shovel it in and needed to be reminded to chew. Tori was the same way, fast and giggling the whole time.

The next couple of days are going to be low-key, as we start to establish a normal routine. The twins are taking a nap now, and we will stay home and hang out the next few days. I am slowly resuming my efforts to get the house ready for the party. Grandma and Papa are coming back in the morning to finish the swing set. I bet they love on the kids too, what ya think?

Again we want to thank all of you for the love, support, and well wishes. We are very lucky to have the kids, and the kids are lucky to have you! Hope we can see you at the party. If you need the address just email me for the address.

Thanks Tom, Sonya, Tori, plus 2

30. Down to business 6/1/10

I just wanted to give a quick update. The kids have adjusted well to their new surroundings and continue to cause a lot of smiles here. They have played in the yard, on the swing set, in the pool and have taken turns beating up Daddy. I happen to love that part.

The boy will be playing the part of informer. Anytime anyone does anything, he is going to tell Mom. Way too cute for words. He also loves to tackle you, when you least expect it. He currently has two speeds, full throttle and avoiding sleep. You can identify the latter by the lack of smile.

The girl, on the other hand, will be our daredevil. She has no fear, and also likes to play hard. While her cd was playing today, we had a dance-off which she won. Her little butt was rocking to the beat, and Sonya and I loved the show. She was singing along in her own world just having a blast.

Tomorrow is a very big day. Do you know what it is??? Well.... Our son and daughter turn three years old, and we are very happy to celebrate. I am not sure what will happen, but I know for sure there will be laughter, hugs, kisses and love. All three of my kids make every day special and rewarding. We are so blessed and so very happy.

We still have a lot to do. Today, I finally sorted the clothes the kids came with into the "yes" and "no" piles. We are sending a lot of clothes to the center as they are too small or winter clothes. We also are scheduling the doctor and dentist appointments. So over the next few days we will get all of the appointments scheduled, finish getting the house ready, meet with the adoption and new beginnings caseworkers, and have a huge welcome home/birthday party.

The next post will provide a lot more detail from the party. Thank you again for taking the time to read this.

Tom, Sonya, Tori and plus 2 :-)

31. Hey kids, welcome to the family..... 6/7

Over the last week we have spent every waking moment playing with the kids, or putting the finishing touches on the house to be ready for the party. Just a couple of quick updates, the twins have adjusted to home very well; they own this place and the grandparents too. We have met with their therapist; she will help with their transition, and the adoption caseworker. The adoption process has begun and will take the next several months. The people at the center has been most helpful in putting up with me over a couple of items, and I say, "Thank you."

The welcome home / birthday party
– A SPECIAL THANK YOU TO AUNT DAWN AND AUNT ERIKA FOR PUTTING IT TOGETHER

The morning of the party started really early. My Mom and Dad spent the night before to "help with the kids," and allow us to work on the setup. Dad was out in the yard at 6 a.m. starting to put up the multiple canopies borrowed for the day. We put up six, some easy and a couple that required the use of some words that will not be repeated here. Let's say that the father in A Christmas Story has nothing on us. We finished that, roped off parking, setup the games, tables and chairs, etc. Mom, Tori and Sonya were working away on the final touches on the inside of the house.

Erika, Dawn, Autumn, Mackenna and Kayla showed up and started with the decorations and food prep. Between the people that said yes and maybe we were at about one hundred people that could show up. Finally noon arrived and we caught our breath for about thirty seconds before the guests started to arrive. We forced the kids to take a short early nap knowing that madness would soon ensue.

When Sonya and I started this journey it was for selfish reasons. We wanted another baby. I didn't worry about how easily the child would be welcomed by our family or friends. I knew the child would be treated well, but I didn't know if the love would be felt as quickly for adopted kids as for a newborn into the group. This blog and the support received from it washed away any concerns long ago. However, I was not prepared for what happened on Saturday.

As people started arriving, my youngest daughter started to wake up from her nap, which can last up to an hour before the smile is glued into place. My son, on the other hand, had delayed falling asleep and showed no sign of life. The poor little guy was just worn out. By the time he finally woke up there were already 10-15 people here. So we started making the rounds. Introductions, smiles, hugs and kisses all over the place. The kids were doing great, seeming to feed off of being the center of attention. The older kids were swimming and the adults hung out on the driveway (ignoring the canopies we worked so hard putting up LOL).

I don't know how many people were here and cannot pretend to say that I talked to everyone. We had aunts, uncles, cousins and extended family and friends from all over the place. A couple of our Children's Center friends showed up, Nashae and Bobby. They were immediately welcomed into the family, and I know a few people thanked them for their help so far. I do know it was a fun time had by all. Many people lost their hearts to the kids in a very short order. I am sorry to all the ladies in attendance as my son was working it, stealing hearts and kisses along the way. I see trouble in my future with that one LOL. Both my girls were having fun and playing games with everyone.

This was an emotional day for a lot of us, a celebration of the love of these great kids and memories of all the ups and downs so far that led to it. My mother, wife and I (there were others that I will not sell out here) teared up a few times while generally overwhelmed with joy and love while telling stories of the first few days in the family. For instance, the moment that Sissy read them a bedtime story. The way they follow her around and how much she loves it. The funny games we play with each other and the laughs we share every hour.

My Mom gets the golden kick in the butt award for making me cry the most. She told me that she wrapped their present, because she was not sure if they have ever ripped open a present before. Yep the water works started pretty good. Not to fear, they are gift-unwrapping experts now. OMG the outpouring of gifts was insane! Their gifts completely buried my king-sized bed, not covered, but buried it (this is after the gifts were opened and consolidated). They got a ton of clothes, cool toys, a personal pool and personal bean bags. We took all day Sunday sorting and finding homes for it all.

At 9 p.m. as the last guests left, the twins finally went down for the night. They must have eaten a ton of food from everyone's plates, not to mention the full plates they each had for dinner.

They are now awake so I am off to play. I will provide another update later this week. Thank you all for a great party and taking the time to read this.
Tom, Sonya, Tori plus 2

32. Getting back to normal 6/12/10

Well the party was a hit; the kids were spoiled with love and gifts. Everyone let them get away with murder, and then they left us with the clean up. Fellow parents please help me understand why one day of sugar and not hearing the word "no" can impact the next few days. LOL! I call it the grandparent effect, where the grandparent returns the kid with no nap, hopped up on sugar and cranky. Then the parents spend the next few days getting the kid back into a normal routine, with the child fighting the entire way.

The welcome home / birthday party was of our own making. We wanted the kids to have a great time, and they did. But the week that followed was so much fun for us. The kids were cranky and not interested in any form of sleep. Then the poor things started cutting teeth (yes, both of them). Even like this they are so much fun, but check back in a few months and see if this story has not changed. Make no mistake; our house is fully alive and jumping all the time.

As my leave from the office nears an end I am getting bummed. I love the work and the people I work with, yet I will go nuts missing these kids. I just love watching them discover and try new things. For instance, our boy will try a new food item with the most nervous look on his face and his eyes firmly closed. Then while chewing he peeks out and shakes his head to show his approval. I am laughing now just thinking about it and am determined to get a video of it soon. Our girl has taken to dancing when a good song comes on the radio, that little butt just wiggling while her face is showing the widest of smiles. I will miss my regular time with Tori. I am making the most of this by driving her to school every day allowing us to talk, plan and giggle.

We have had our second meeting with the transition therapist; she is helping with great ideas on ways to help the kids adjust. Their caseworker stopped by to check in, and our adoption worker is completing the required updates to the paperwork. She is completing addendums to our licensing forms to include the adoption details, the kid's documentation to show that they have now been placed, and she is checking our references.

The way I understand the process is that when the addenda are complete a request can be submitted to the State Superintendent, the person who is legally responsible for all children in the State's care. He will review the request and all of the details. If he agrees that it is a good fit, he will approve the placement. The approval could take a few months. Then we are waiting on subsidy information. Foster care parents are provided a small daily allowance to assist in the care and needs of the children. Because the twins are three they will get assistance through age of 18. If the adoption occurred prior to their birthday there would be no future state aide. Because of this ongoing support special forms are needed. The State is doing everything they can to ensure the children are positioned well for the future. The entire process will take some time but we are very happy to go through the steps.

The next few days are going to be full of research; we need to find support for several areas including additional training on hair care, and area activities in the area that may help the kids. We will keep you updated.
Thanks for your time
Tom, Sonya, Tori plus 2

33. Back at the grind 6/18/10

Well the honeymoon is over. As Tori started her summer vacation, I had to return to work. For my last day of freedom I decided that all five of us should go get our medical forms updated for the State. This was the first journey to the doctor with the twins. I am happy to report that handled it like any other three-year-olds. They were fine until the doctor walked into the room, and then the water works began. Everyone is fine, and we are good to go.

The twins are taking great pride in testing the boundaries of their new home. I had forgotten how funny and frustrating this stage can be. Just last night, a half hour after being tucked in, the boy decided it was time to run giggling through the entire main floor. Not realizing that sound traveled and that Mom has ears that actually work, he was very surprised when caught in the middle of the second lap. I almost died from suppressing a laugh when Mom was in mid-lecture and he took off giggling again. After being caught a second time and facing the firing squad he went back to bed. At this point the show was over, so I decided to play the currently paused television program. You can imagine the surprise when he showed up at the foot of the bed; this time acting like it was the morning and he wanted to watch TV with us. I know, too darn funny. For those of you that are parents, yes he went back to bed, and this time feel asleep without visiting the dreaded "Time-Out Corner," which does hold power with these two.

Now the funny part of this story is that the little girl pulled a similar stunt during nap time the day before. That one ended with me picking her up and carrying her into our room. That little "Angel" looked me dead in the eye as I placed her on the king size bed and said, "Dad's not playing now." I wanted to laugh so hard but instead walked around the bed and lay down next to her until she fell asleep. It is a good thing they are so cute.

However, the greatest joy right now is watching Tori. She comes up to me to complain about something one of the kids did. Oh, to see the stunned look in her face when I explain how she did the very same thing on some level that week! Of course I tell her it is the normal process of growing up. Her eyes get really big and she says, "Oh," and I just could lose it. Being the great kid that she is, she is helping any way she can. This includes leading by example after these talks. The best big sister ever!!!

We are currently working with The center to submit all the paperwork to the State. Meanwhile, we are moving forward as a family, loving and being grateful for every day.
More of the same, yet it seems so different 6/27
Another week has passed, far too quickly I might add. Tori spent her first week of freedom going to day camp with her Girl Scout friends. She had a blast and discovered she is pretty good with a bow. If the first couple weeks of the summer are any indication, we are in for a real treat watching her grow by leaps and bounds. She is trying new things, taking on new responsibilities and gaining more confidence every day. This is truly an amazing show to watch.

The twins are also quite the show. They have been testing boundaries in major ways. You ask them to do something, they say no. You put them in the corner, they say no, or shut up. As parents you fight to keep the line steady to reinforce the rules. So every day is crime and punishment, crime and punishment, and then crime, frustration and punishment. After a while you feel like all you are doing is fighting with the kids and start to question if it will ever end. Sonya and I even ask are we being too tough on them (all three). Then just when you are sure nothing will change, it does. You see little wins pop up. The kid responds in the desired way when threatened with time out. You can teach one to take a break and deep breath when frustrated (way to go Sonya).

In addition to the wins, you also see light at the end of the tunnel. At age three our twins are learning by leaps and bounds every day. In true kid fashion they will not do any of the following if asked, but we know they can. They can count to ten in English, and I have been teaching them Spanish (with some help from Dora). Swiper NO swiping! LOL (not many of you got that one). They enjoy puzzles and are very good at them, unless they want to play with all of them at the same time.

We were provided a copy of the files on the kids. This includes their known medical and social background. We sat here and read every document. We know more than ever about the kids and are so happy they are here with us. I won't share any of the details here, but the files have been very helpful and informative.

Parenting tricks and tips
- Label puzzles and pieces to support easy sorting when they mix them all up. In our house each puzzle equals a letter and each piece get a letter and number. The back of the puzzle get the letter and total number of pieces listed on it in marker (thanks Mom).

- I fear teenage daughters. The therapy is helping, and I have starting planning for Tori. Sonya and I have found the show "World's Strictest Parents" on CMT. This show provides some great ideas on how to set and enforce rules for children of all ages. Ok, they don't work on me (for all my friends).

- We are working with the twins on speech. They mispronounce a few commonly-used words. We are teaching then the correct pronunciation, and then practicing. After about a week we start prompting for self-correction with, "What is the right word?" We give them lots of praise when they get the words right.

PLEASE COMMENT WITH ANY OTHER SUGGESTED TIPS FOR WORKING WITH CHILDREN THROUGH FUN LEARNING EXCERCISES. I will credit you with the idea and create a page of reader tips. This could be fun and informative.

As for the adoption, a lot of progress has been made there too. Our wonderful caseworkers have completed about 80% of the paperwork. There will be two areas of focus for this waiting period. First, we have submitted our adoption request to the state superintendant and we are waiting for his approval. The second focus area requires us to wait on another department in Lansing. We assume we will be waiting several months before we can get in front of the judge.

34. Special Moments... 7/17/10

I am sorry I have not updated lately, and yes, I have a lot to report. Here are some highlights of the last 3 weeks.
Just this week we were provided with a wonderful update. All of the information has been sent to the superintendant in Lansing. We need his blessing before getting in front of the judge for the adoption. He normally takes around forty-five days to review the application. Yep, that's right - we are waiting again. I confess it is a lot easier to wait now that we get to see these little bundles of joy every day.

We also have had some really special times, those magic moments where the stars align and burn a point in time into your memory forever.
-Today on the way home from the museum, Tori sat in the backseat between the twins and was teaching them how to spell their full names.
-About a week ago, all five of us were watching the Disney channel while lying in our suddenly small king-sized bed. It was heaven; I looked up to Sonya and confessed that I can't remember life before they got here.
-The days when you play so hard they look at you and announce, "I tired." The parent can sometimes see the clouds part and hear angels sing at this moment.
-Seeing the kids falling in love with their new family.
-My son and I being put in the corner... Yeah, what of it? I said, "damn it," and he repeated it. So we did time together and then apologized.

Everything is wonderful these days. They are normal three-year-olds, testing every rule in the book. Yet, the smiles, laughs, hugs, kisses and moments like those are what I love about being a parent. We still have a lot to do before family reunion. I will keep you updated if anything changes.

Thank you again for your time and support.
Tom, Sonya and all 3 kids.

35. We continue to learn... 8/8/10

In the last month you have not missed much from the adoption process; however, you have missed a lot from the bonding process. We are very happy having the twins at home; they know it, and they show it. Our little girl was feeling saucy and tried to put Mom in the corner. Yeah, that didn't work. I love her for trying it, I was laughing for hours. Each day is a blessing, and we are most thankful to have them in the family. I know I keep saying this and will continue to do so.

Today we met another member of our adoption team. The twins have a court-appointed attorney. We found out that he has been with our kids since birth. His job is to make sure the kids' best interests are looked after. He partners with our adoption worker as we progress. We had a great visit at my Mom and Dad's house; the attorney explained where we are in the current process.

The paperwork has been sent to the two offices necessary for review. From there, if approved, we will then start the process to get in front of the judge. At this point the attorney thinks we are like a year away from it being final. Which is okay – the twins are home and are well worth the wait (as those of you that have got to meet them know). We were informed that there is a quarterly review in court where the twins are discussed, and the progress towards adoption is tracked. This is good. The next visit the attorney will come out to the house.

We also shared part of our story with him, and there is a good chance that he will read this post too (hello). He was able to shed a little more light into their past. He was pleased with the comfort level of the kids and said some nice things that were very encouraging. While talking with him, you can't help but feel nervous. All of the adoption team has been with these kids for years and are totally committed to their well-being. We are so happy to see others caring for them as we do. We are the new players. We are the ones that need to prove our worth and love for these two wonderful kids.

The next few weeks are going to be very busy from the family perspective. First we are going to the county fair this week and to a children's music review by Broadway stars. Follow that up the following week with our first family vacation with the twins, a long weekend at Great Wolf Lodge. The plan is to wear all three of them out and try to survive in the process~ LOL. Then the following week, unknown to the twins, they will actually get to ride on Thomas the Train. Yep, we will be Super mom and Super dad by September. I hope to get Tori's new room painted by then too. So if you don't hear from me....

Thanks again for your time. Tom, Sonya, Tori plus 2

36. Our First Family Vacation 8/22/10

Lets recap.. The kids have been with us for almost four months. Everything to this point has been an introduction into their new life. We have introduced them to their grandparents, a party with a ton of family and friends, the house, their rooms and our pets. We have tried to take baby steps (pardon the pun) to not overload the kids in our efforts to ease them into this crazy family. Every step of the way the twins have done great, accepting every new thing with a smile and laughter that warms the heart.

We have been planning a short trip for a few months prior to the twins' arrival. We were kicking around the idea of going to a family reunion in Tennessee. That trip just didn't work out. However when the twins came home we were planning a back-up vacation, a few days at Great Wolf Lodge (Tori's claims it is a, "Kick-butt water park"). We had learned with Tori to delay announcing the vacation as long as possible for the sanity of Mom and Dad. The sooner you spill the beans, the crazier the build-up until they are ready to explode with excitement.

As the magic day got closer, we struggled to keep the secret. We let Tori know in advance, because she was bummed about missing the Tennessee trip. Just like with any vacation, there are always ten million things that need to be done prior to heading out. One of the big ones was to get the twins set up for school. They will attend school four days a week during the school year and get to ride the bus (very cool and yes they are excited). Sonya was nominated to be a representative on the Lapeer County's Parent Advisory Committee for Special Education. She accepted the nomination, and I am so very proud of and excited for her.

Finally the night before our vacation arrived. We told the kids we would be going on vacation and need a good night's sleep. They quickly got baths and were tucked in for the night. We planned a normal morning, with all of us heading out shortly after breakfast. Before the kids woke up, we had everything packed and stacked at the back door. I went to drop off the dogs and at their retreat. When I returned home the twins were waking up, just as happy as could be. That is until our youngest daughter saw the suitcases and then even worse, she saw her toys and clothes going into some of them. She frantically shook her from side to side and kept saying, "NO." It didn't take long for our son to pick up on this, and poof! We had our hands full. We soon realized they thought they were leaving us and not that the family was going somewhere together. Sonya and I each held one and tried to explain the concept of a vacation, while trying to get them to eat at the same time. Finally breakfast was done. They were still nervous, but we headed out.

Traverse City's Great Wolf Lodge was just four short hours away. I would like to take a minute here and thank the inventor of the portable DVD player! Whoever you are, thank you!!! The kids watched Ice Age (forever known in my house as the elephant movie). At about the half way point we found a park and had a family picnic lunch, then off the rest of the way. We just made it through Disney's Brother Bear as we were pulling into the parking lot of the hotel. At this point the kids were back to normal and very excited walking through the door. After stopping for a few quick photos, we shot up to the room for a quick change and then to dinner and the pool.

The look on their little faces was unreal as we started exploring the water park. After about thirty seconds the games began. We were walking through waterfalls, shooting large squirt guns at each other, going down the toddler water slides and wading in the water. Tori was off to stand under the big bucket that would empty on the nuts, I mean people, waiting three stories below. She was also running between the four different water slides, stopping by to only check in.

We spent the last ten minutes of our first night in the hot tub. Both of the twins we laying back floating in the water with really heavy eyes. We decided to head back to the room. I asked my son if he would like to swim again tomorrow. "Do it one more time," (that is how it sounded) was his response. We got back to the room and got ready to spend the night. We had a blast swimming the following day away. They both went under the water and jumped from the side of the pool in our arms. My oldest daughter did try to kill me on this trip. We went on one waterslide together. The put us on a two seat inner-tube and launched down this enclosed tube. OMG!!!! We were moving really fast through five sharp turns that made you fear flipping over and out of the tube. Finally we hit the bottom and hydroplaned across the water. She was laughing so hard that my having heart pound through my chest seemed worth it. But I will never do it again.

So our first family vacation with the twins is in the book and we all had a great time. We barely made it home and everyone needed a nap. Even now, the next day, we are still moving in slow motion. Now, next weekend's adventure will involve a ride on Thomas the Train, who has rock star status in our house. Should be a blast!

Thanks again for taking the time to read this.
Tom, Sonya, Tori plus 2

37. What a week... 9/4/10

As Barney says, "There are seven days, there are seven days, there are seven days in a week." We had just returned from Great Wolf Lodge, where my three lovely children tried to drown me. The cute little angels began the week like any other kid would return from vacation by making Mom and Dad pay for showing them a good time. Fighting every decision, nap, bath and of course each other during the first couple of days home.

As the following weekend approached we kept our plans quiet. On Friday, thinking back to the dreaded suitcase experience, I informed the kids of our pending visit to see Thomas the Train. We had a full day riding Thomas, hanging out with Sir Tophamhatt and Percy, and then we got to spend some time with Bob the Builder. Yep, we all had a great day. Sissy had a good day. At times you could see the struggle between the little girl and pre-teen, each trying to take control during the experience. When it was all said and done she had fun and enjoyed being there.

Then on Wednesday the world lost a very special person, Sonya's Grandma Shirkey lost her fight with cancer, leaving behind a huge loving and spiritual family as her legacy. For those of you that have followed our journey from the beginning you may recall, that we started this adoption journey at a funeral for a loved one, Grandpa Snodgrass pointed us in the right direction and the center. Now Grandma Shirkey pushed us forward, when on Thursday we were informed that the state superintendant approved our request to adopt the twins. This means that we are one court date away from the paperwork being complete.

Reflecting back on this journey to this point we are blessed. Our guardian angels have led us here and continue to provide guidance. Knowing this is only the beginning of a wonderful lifetime adventure, we have to thank everyone for their love and support. Our twins have learned their new last name, and take pride in telling you about it.

Thanks again for taking the time to read this.
Tom, Sonya, Tori plus 2

38. Establishing the new routine 9/12/10

Before you ask, we have not heard any news on the court date. I can confirm that the paperwork is being filed and the date should come soon. As promised when allowed, I will post a picture so everyone can see the entire family.

In Michigan September signals many things, we have cooler temperatures coming, the leaves will change colors in one of the most spectacular shows Mother Nature will put on for us. The fresh apple cider and sugar donuts begin to call you, bonfires are required and parents rejoice as kids complain with the start of the new school year.

Tori started 5th grade, her last year in this school before she moves over to middle school. As my previous post show the twins have adjusted to the new surroundings and relationships better than I could have ever hoped. Even with that track record, I was a little nervous as the twins were to start preschool this past week.

We have had little chances to see if the twins would be okay, with neither of us around. Yet, nothing prepared Sonya for what happened on Wednesday morning. The twins were very upset, not because they were going to school. Nope, they were mad because Mom was taking them to school and they couldn't ride the bus. When all three of them arrived in the class room, the teacher shared a horror story of kids crying in the morning. Not ours, they looked right at her and said, "Bye Mom." Now the funny part of this whole story is that Mom was more upset over the first day (being dismissed) then they were attending class.

Now I know what you are thinking and don't worry... the kids were able to ride the bus the next day. Kids just seem to find new ways to amaze and humble you at the same time. Yes, there is a reason they are so cute, it makes it easier for us to cope!

Have a great week and thank you again for taking the time to join us on this journey.
Tom, Sonya, Tori plus 2

39. The emotional roller coaster from hell... 9/18/10

To all of my close friends that tease me about being a big softy. I freely admit it here for the world to see, that you are right and I am wrong. I have told many of you that this blog is a form of therapy for me, it has helped me analyze my emotions and then to face them head on. But nothing prepared me for this one...

Now before I tell you what happened this past Thursday, let me explain the since the kids came to join us (May 28th) I have lived in fear. Every day I hope the adoption becomes final, so I know my kids are here to stay. Every bump or bruise makes my heart skip a beat. It's not any different than with Tori; I am just an overprotective parent.

While waiting for a meeting to start at work, I got a text message telling me that my son says the beagle has bitten him. I freaked! I jumped up, excusing myself and leaving the room. I had to call home. When Sonya answered she was calm, and the twenty questions game started. By the end of the call I knew that my son was in the living room with the dog, while my wife was in the kitchen. He came to her crying with a red mark on his face and saying the dog bit him.

This dog plays with and kisses all of the kids; she has never done anything like this in her life. In her entire three years with us she has been surrounded by kids. I knew all of this, yet in less than a second said she had to go.

We knew what was needed. We had to make sure he was okay and inform the caseworkers... My mind was racing, playing heck with my fears. All I could think of was losing the kids and having to fight for them. While trying to walk to the next meeting, I fought tears (lost that one) and felt the panic, weighing as much as a house, sitting on my chest.

The more I tried to calm myself the worse the images flashing through my head became. If the twins are taken away, how do I get them to understand what is happening? How can I make this okay for them? How do I explain all of this to Tori? I was in a personal hell falling further with each minute.

I work with amazing people that not only understood I was hurting, but they went out of their way to comfort and encourage me to head home to my family. By the time I agreed, I was in the midst of a full-fledged panic attack. Just the thought of someone taking my kids then (and reliving it now) ripped my heart out. I have no words to describe this hurt.

Trying to calm myself during the ride home, I called Sonya. Hearing that our son was fine and that the small marks were clearing up did nothing for me. The fact that she was only able to leave messages with our caseworkers gave my mind some extra time to put me through the wringer.

When I got home the marks on his face were now "the mark," and it looked like a scratch by his eye. He was not able to tell us what happened, but we know he uses the word bite to describe a lot of things. To be safe, Sonya had the dog in her kennel. Both my son and the dog were acting like nothing happened. My son responded with, "yeah," when asked if it was her teeth or paw that got him.

I assume some of you are saying, "Way to overreact. Everyone knows how great you are with those kids." Well let me tell you, child safety is the primary concern of their entire team (as it should be). A dog bite could equate to an unsafe environment and the risk of the kids being taken, although the worst case scenario, is and was very real.

In the living room, Sonya and I sat in silence as the kids and dogs played as nothing happened. Each fighting tears, at the thoughts running through our heads. I was worried about what would happen with the caseworkers and trying to come to grips with getting rid of a great dog. Pet owners will tell you that pets are like their kids and I agree, but this dog was gone. If I HAD to choose between the dog and the kids, this was a no brainer. Then the ringing phone forced us back to the moment. It was our adoption caseworker; she was coming out to get the adoption papers signed. I informed her of everything that had happened, and she said a couple of things that sent off bells and whistles for me, "I don't know how the other caseworker will handle this," and "I am still going to come out and get the papers signed." She said we were doing everything the way we were supposed to, by reaching out right away and she suggested just to be safe take him to be seen by the doctor.

I stayed home with my youngest daughter to wait for the caseworker, and Sonya took our son to urgent care. In the course of those ninety minutes, the house that was weighing on my chest turned into a skyscraper apartment complex as the panic held onto me. Our youngest daughter played while I was folding clothes, trying to do anything to distract myself. Finally, as a last ditch effort, I called a friend to virtually hold my hand while waiting for whatever was next, thank you Darlene and Donna (I think it was Donna).

Finally Sonya showed up. Our son was wired as he got a red sucker, and everyone knows that red suckers are the best. The doctor reported that the mark was not a bite, but rather a scratch, as none of the signs of a bite were present. At this point that little spot by his eye was totally unnoticeable unless you knew where to look.

Shortly after hearing that news our caseworker showed up with the adoption packets (one for each kid). She got her hugs, looked at him and told us we shouldn't worry. One down, two caseworkers to go I thought. We sat around the table, all three in an emotional state. She has been with the kids their entire life and was really happy they were with us and were going to stay. We told stories, laughed and cried happy tears. I am so very happy she wants to stay connected in the kids' life. There are a lot of people at the center that have asked for this connection. We want them to stay connected. We want to add to the kids' loved ones and not take anyone away from them.

As we sat there signing papers and discussing the kids, I was still a wreck waiting on the other caseworkers to call. They were all very supportive and understanding. The doctor's report and visual report from our caseworker helped ease any tension that may have existed over the phone. I know when I heard the word bite I came up with horrible visuals in my head. The caseworkers will come out next week to file the required report. At that time we will decide together if we need to find a home for Lucy the beagle. To my surprise my mom and dad are willing to be a temporary home until we can find a full time home. All of us, including the twins are very attached to Lucy; we are keeping a close eye on her. The twins still play with and kiss her, so I hope it's a non-issue.

Now knowing that the kids are staying, I was hoping I would feel some relief but it did not come. I was still in panic mode while signing our way through the paperwork. We signed the last couple of pages and my brain started to fire again. I asked how long it will take until we get our court date. She told us that a court date is not needed. The judge will sign the papers, and one day we will get a call telling us the adoption is final. I walked her out as she left to go to the courthouse and file the paperwork. I have to thank everyone at the center for helping us and putting up with my million questions through this entire process.

In the course of one hour long conversation we went from hell to heaven, from tears of pain and fear to shock and joy. I was so out of it that I failed to ask about timing, so we will all be surprised when it happens. I am pretty sure I lost ten years with all of the emotion felt that day. To be honest I am still trying to recover. But the kids have the sniffles and normalcy will have to wait and return later.

I will let you know when we get news. As this adoption story nears its conclusion (only the adoption, there is a lifetime of fun ahead for us), I want to thank you from the bottom of my heart for your time and support.
Tom, Sonya, Tori plus 2

40. A new beginning or two..... 10/2/10

We started down this path over a year ago, much of the time between now and then of our own making. The last five months have been super-fast spurts followed by waiting periods. After the emotional roller coaster of the alleged dog bite and then signing adoption papers, I needed a quiet week to recharge the batteries. I was so drained emotionally; I walked through life as a zombie for two days while working to recover.

Then a week later I realized that I had to get ready for my first public speaking appearance. A dear, sweet friend, Holly (the same one that convinced me to create this blog) had requested I speak to her social media class about my blog. I had no clue as to why, but what the heck. I could tell more people about foster care and the center. We scheduled the presentation for Wednesday, September 29, 2010. As time approached I created a PowerPoint and decided I would speak from the heart with no formal words prepared.

We have also restarted the home improvement projects working on Tori's new room. Thankfully the drywall mud is done and the sanding will be finished today. Finishing my last three classes for my degree has become an exercise in self motivation, but I will be done in nine short weeks. The kids have been doing great. Tori's first progress report came back with huge improvements over last year. Alex and Alaya are both loving school and are trying to grow out of the nap stage, with little success.

What? "Alex and Alaya?" you say. Oh yeah! On Wednesday, September 29, 2010, we received notice that the adoption has entered into supervision mode. This means the adoption is court approved. The kids are ours and yes home, forever! So allow me to introduce you to Alexander and Alaya, our two new beautiful additions. We are very blessed and very happy. The adoption will be final after they have been in the home for six months. This means we will have the caseworkers continuing to come to the house until November. I want to take this time to say a big special thank you to all our friends at the center! Your help and support has been amazing and inspiring.

I was informed of the wonderful news fifteen minutes before I was to leave for that speaking appearance. The entire hour-plus ride was spent on the phone talking with loved ones and sharing the great news. While at home Sonya and Tori shared happy tears while playing with the twins. It was a celebration. The rest of the day was a dream that even now a few days later I don't want to end. The presentation was unreal; everyone was so welcoming and engaged that my presentation became a conversation. I had such a great time! I would jump at the chance to do it again.

Now comes the part where I need your help. With the adoption soon to be final, I think a logical conclusion to end this journey would be the end of year. I'll post until we get through the paperwork and have our first holiday season together. Others have told me to keep going or start a new blog that follows us through childhood. I am not sure and would welcome your thoughts.

Thank you again for your time,
Tom, Sonya, Tori, Alex and Alaya.

41. Ending this chapter.... 10/8/10

This update is going to be very self-serving. I have mentioned my intention to create a book for the kids. This post will be the last entry in the book. I will get three copies made and close this portion. For those of you who have voiced your desire for me to keep going, thank you and I will. This site will continue to be updated, just not in the book. Knowing this I ask for your understanding with the following open letter to my children

To my wonderful children,
I am writing this letter to you in the hopes that many years from now you can really understand how special this time in our lives has been.

Tori, you are the most amazing person I know. You are so smart and are destined to do well in whatever you choose. Your warm heart is your biggest asset. I hope you know how very proud of you we are. We have had so much fun watching you grow into the young woman you are now, and we are looking forward to watching your journey continue. We are so happy that you are finally a big sister, and we are proud of the way you fill that role. The kids already idolize you. The example you are setting is wonderful. I love you, little girl, forever and always.

Alaya and Alex, you have been with us now for only five months, and we know you are here to stay. Every day since your arrival has been a gift for us. Your wonderful welcoming spirits along with your giggles fill us with pride and warmth that cannot be described. We are so happy our family is now complete. Welcome to your home! I promise to love and protect you both to the best of my ability beyond my last breath. I made this same promise to your big sister almost eleven years ago in a hospital room. Many people tell us that we did a great thing by adopting you. The fact is, my angels, that you are the gift to us.

I hope that years from now when you three are married and maybe even have kids of you own that you realize how very special our team is. Your brother or sisters will always be there for you, your kids and your family. Your mom and dad will be here to love you, support you, and most likely annoy you to the point you want to put us in a home. We are starting our next leg of this journey together. We are one team, one group with a common love and common goals and we are off. Don't rush, let's take our time and enjoy each and every step.

Love,
Dad

UPDATE: The Story Continues… 3/22/13

The twins are will turn six in a few months and things are still magical here. They have tested out of special needs pre-school and are doing well within "traditional kindergarten." Both were recently diagnosed with ADHD, as was their big sister.

Their personalities continue to shine, and Sonya and I are still thankful every single day for all of our kids. Tori continues to develop into a strong young woman, 13 now, and is amazing with the twins. We continue to explore life as a trans-racial family and are happy to have one another.

The blog still lives (http://thankyoufostercare.blogspot.com) and we share all of our ups and downs. I only hope that it will help one other kid in foster care be adopted into a loving family.

Thank you for your time.
Tom

7224741R00064

Made in the USA
San Bernardino, CA
27 December 2013